AF566743

HOLYPOL

RAJBIR DESWAL

## About the Book

This is first compilation of middles written by Rajbir Deswal and published in national dailies like The Tribune, The Hindustan Times, The Indian Express and The Pioneer.

HOLYPOL opens up vistas that are captivating and compel indulgence of sorts on the part of the reader. Imagine a Police System up there in Heavens! Visualize the Lady of the House breaking crystals while the domestic help grins! Experience your straying into a Chor Bazaar! Marvel at the amount of discretion the Americans give to their lower level functionaries! See a thousand Medallions on your chest! Show up your best image to the rest of the world after a makeup of style! Dot on Balcony in a building being symbol of concrete liberty. Hear the spinning of yarn by Journo lap wing seeking to regain her eggs! Experience the Withdrawal symptoms in a New Year! Listen to Speaking tree's clamoring for green cover! Watch bedlam in a Divided House where windows and curtains fight for one-up man-ship! Step into the shoes of co-sufferers but only when disasters strike! Heed to the Call of the Unknown Soldier! Walk on the brittle sheet of water! Enjoy being caught up in a jam! Experience embarrassing encounters with strangers! Become your wife's conscience-keeper on Karwa Chauth! Know about the pranks played by the Balcony Babbler! Wish your own welfare in blessing others! Decipher that lower lip lingo! Experience the honey-mooning ordeal when faced with the Coast Guard on the beaches of Goa! Look at the guts of the girl flying a plane! Seek seasonal favours due from Government Departments and experience discomfiture! Find Flowery Epaulets on the shoulders of a subdued cop! Experience an airport in your bedroom! Watch out for that vanity in your darling motor cars! Argue on out-stepping BSF boys and Pakistani rangers at Wagah! Place trust in the Song of Promise! Be a Chosen One in the Almighty's scheme of things! Look at the likeness of the moment with the Man! Share the plight of those who need to be sent to Coventry being discarded! Listen to the agony of the Enigmatic Driver who is a father too! See More than what meets the eye ! Find the difference between real happiness and faked one! Watch sleeping women lie ! Hear for whom the bell tolls, being tricked into a bizarre predicament! Get thrown overboard with offers of days and nights to be spent in a foreign country as part of promos! Get at the meaning of a two fingered comment ! Estimate if you are Tana-tunn in health or otherwise ! Lend your ear to the Bar counsel ! Be pen(ny)-wise ! Solve mysteries of Blue! Advise Olympian Vijender to choose from amongst the Bollywood girls ! Look out for a suitable dog for the Obamas.

And find much more hereafter in HOLYPOL.

**Write in the Middle: I**

# HOLYPOL

RAJBIR DESWAL

DK's BOOKS FOR ALL

Delhi 110 052

Author: Rajbir Deswal

© Mrs. Chander Koumdi

Published 2010

ISBN 10: 81-7386-281-8
ISBN 13: 978-81-7386-281-6

**Published by:**
DK's BOOKS FOR ALL
A-6, Nimri Commercial Centre,
Ashok Vihar Phase-IV, Delhi 110 052
Ph.: +91-11-2730 2453 Fax.: +91-11-4706 1936
e-mail: booksforall@Lppindia.com
website: -www.booksforall.Lppindia.com

Printed at
D K Fine Art Press P Ltd.
Delhi 110 052

No part of this book may be reproduced, stored in or introduced into a retrieval system, or transmitted in any form or by any means (electronic, mechanical, photocopying, recording or otherwise), without the prior written permission of the above mentioned publisher of this book.

PRINTED IN INDIA

*TO ANAYSA*

## Contents

KHUSHWANT SINGH

49-E, SUJAN SINGH PARK
NEW DELHI - 110003

30 Dec. 2009

I have known Rajbir Deswal for some years in different incarnations. First as a young police officer interested in literature. He insisted I invite him to all my book launches. I did & he came from wherever he was posted in Haryana. I did not realise he harboured literary ambitions and hoped that one day in the very near future he would launching his own books before gatherings of the literati. He achieved that with collections of humorous episodes of Haryanvi humour in its own dialect. Soon instead of him reading my books, I was reading his.

Then he launched on writing middles for national newspapers like The Hindustan Times, The Tribune, The Indian Express & The Pioneer. He has made a name for himself as one of the best writers of middles in the country. He is pithy, witty, wields a light pen and writes on a baffling variety of subjects. I make it a point to read everything he writes.

Above all things Rajbir Deswal is a policeman as well as a polished gentleman — a combination rarely found in India of today

Khushwant Singh

# Foreword

KHUSHWANT SINGH

49-E, SUJAN SINGH PARK
NEW DELHI-110003

30th Dec, 2009

I have known Rajbir Deswal for some years in different incarnations. First, as a young police officer interested in literature. He wanted me to invite him to all my book launches I did. He came from wherever he was posted in Haryana. I did not realise he harboured literary ambitions and hope that one day in the very near future he would be launching his own books before gatherings of the literati. He achieved that with collections of humorous episodes of Haryanvi Humour in its own dialect. Soon, instead of him reading my books, I was reading his.

Then he launched on witty middles for national newspapers like The Hindustan Times, The Tribune, The Indian Express and The Pioneer. He has made a name for himself as one of the best writers of the middles in the country. He is pithy, witty, wields a light pen and writes on a baffling variety of subjects. I make it a point to read everything he writes.

Above all things Rajbir Deswal is a police officer as well as a polished gentleman—a combination rarely found in India of today.

KHUSHWANT SINGH

# Preface

Those who read newspapers might have noticed a small piece of writing carried at the centre of the opinion page, popularly known as the editorial page. A daily newspaper is considered incomplete without this page. It is the soul of a newspaper. Most of the items, big and small, one finds on this particular page are of a serious nature. Too much seriousness is another name for dullness, and that is why most newspaper readers skip this page. Since the newspaper editor is conscious of this reality, he has found a way to minimise the drabness of the opinion page. He publishes a small but well-written article, appropriately called the "middle", which helps enliven the page.

It is not easy to write "middle". It requires not only the capacity to produce excellent prose, but also an ability to look at life from a different angle, unlike an ordinary writer. If life is full of pathos, it also has a funnier or non-serious side to it. There are situations which deserve sarcastic comment. The newspaper "middle" reflects these and other such aspects of life. In short, it is either a humorous or satirical comment, or just a thoughtful depiction of the lighter side of life.

Rajbir Deswal excels in looking at the vicissitudes of life in this manner. His "middles" provide proof of his uncanny knack of producing highly readable write-ups, which cannot be ignored by a discerning reader. Whatever he writes invariably gets published because he knows what exactly is a good "middle". Deswal has learnt the art of "middle" writing through ceaseless dedication and hard work. He has been in the business of writing for a fairly long time.

"Middle" writing comes naturally to Deswal. That is why he has been churning out such pieces on a regular basis. He has developed a style of his own, which makes his articles highly readable. His felicity with the language is remarkable. He has the capacity to play with the words. His deep knowledge of English literature helps in giving a new and meaningful touch to his writings.

Deswal, being a keen reader of newspapers, is fully aware of the developments in India and the rest of the world. This makes it easier for him to find subjects to covey what he intends to. It is not without reason why he has begun to be rated as one of the top "middle" writers of the country.

Syed Nooruzzaman

# Editor's Note

"Write as you would talk" is what Rajbir Deswal has been following while penning middles published in the leading national dailies for the last twenty years or so. He received his initial training under the famous Tamil critic and English story writer Ka Naa Subramanyam.

Rajbir Deswal already has four widely acclaimed books(Wit & Humour of Haryana; Culture:Bright & Dark; Latke-Jhatke and Taron ke Jungle) to his credit which received rave reviews including at the hands of Mr. Khushwant Singh, Amar Chandel, Randeep Wadhera, Shalini Rawat, Humra Quraishi, and Shiv Kant of BBC.

Holycop is a compilation of about sixty middles out of about five-hundred so far published by Deswal. These culled out middles have a typical class of itself. They generally fit in the categories of philosophy, city-life, human relations, satire, humour, irony, playing pranks, and amusing predicaments. Some happenings marked by their peculiarities on the canvas of time and recent history have been dwelt humorously in some of the middles. The characters in Deswal's middles are very realistic and seem to be coming out of the piece to shake hands with the readers.

Most of the middles in the present compilation relate to a wide range of human predicaments and recent important happenings be it 'selecting a dog for Obamas'; Dating advice of Olympian Vijender; Concern of environment as projected by a 'Speaking Tree'; cornering the better half on the wrong foot when she breaks all imported crystals' with 'clinking cacophony'; and inter alia weaving an encounter with a representative of the Police Force, up in the Heavens—Holypol aptly called Holycop

Rajbir Deswal is known for his punches and ready wit. His by-line with a story compels indulgence. The author is also a regular book reviewer on The Tribune's panel besides being a writer of travelogues and technical articles on Disaster Management, Security Scenario, Negotiations and Communication Skills

The legendary Mr. Khushwant Singh has written the foreword of 'Holypol' which speaks volumes of the tenacity of the author with his passion for writing 'pithy and witty' middles in abundant terms.

Chander Koumdi

# Me the Middleman and my Middles

Common perception is that compiled middles, until and unless have something special in them, cease to belong to all times since they are written to facilitate a daily feed of the edit page with events , situations, atmosphere, environment, characters, ironies, agonies and exuberance of the concurrent times.

It's generally believed that by the time a compilation is conceived and brought out in book form, an element of staleness sets in, to put the reader off, dubbing the middles as a kind of stuff that is recast and recycled; hence it could be relegated to a secondary preference when it came to light reading.

I am saying it here to impress upon the readers that all this in not true. The only requirement to enjoy a middles collection is to travel back in time to the situations and scenarios once obtaining with the middle writer. Synchronise your sensibilities with those of the middle writer, feel as he felt when he penned that piece of pure literature and history—yes it is one—and enjoy it.

In the present compilation—Holypol—in your hands, you need to overlook the element of time and space juxtaposed with your current period, phase or stage. These middles were written at different junctures, legs and holds.

Feelings and impressions are what the middle writers seek to transfer to the readership in the most objective fashion so as to make them identifiable with some kind of a universality of appeal. Hence, the stuff that middles are made up of belong to all times and to all and sundry.

If I have a right to assess myself as a middle writer then let me confess I still am a learner. Self deprecation is the key to letting the readers come along for they do not see a holier-than-thou facade of the middle writer. Nor are they in doing so intimidated by a by-line. Largely I have tried to tickle the funny bone in my creations but the seriousness of thought and understanding things in their appropriate nuances and genres is ingrained in the process of penning them.

I gainsay that I have human-relations, irony, plain humour, satire, situations, atmosphere, environment, society, customs, people, places, incongruities, simplicity, innocuousness, inspiration, philosophy, psychology, history, entertainment, enough Bollywood and much more in my picnic basket. I promise you pleasure of reading folks.

Rajbir Deswal

## Holypol

Trying to work out a case, I felt like scratching my head. I removed my peak-cap and unconsciously rubbed my baton with it. A jinn appeared out of nothing and saluted me.

He introduced himself as the "Holypol cop" and said that they too have a police system up there. "Obviously", I murmured to myself.

To know his rank in relation to mine so that I could immediately establish my seniority or otherwise with him to (en)treat him "befittingly", I asked him his batch.

The "holycop" smiled and declared, while twirling his well-oiled moustaches, that he belonged to the *Satyug* batch. He further revealed that they had other batches also like *Treta* and *Kalyug*. "But our *Kalyug* 'holycops', of late, have developed tendencies what you mortal cops sometimes exhibit", he lamented with an evident contempt in his eyes.

To lighten his disgust, I asked him if they too wear uniforms with long pockets. Perhaps not understanding my mundane mechanics of materialistic magnitude (or feigning innocence, for you never know our tribe), he questioned,

"Why after all do you need long pockets?" I saw his left coffer in the cheek having developed a lump. Realising that my reply could infuriate him further, I changed the topic.

"Holycop, do you also come across these queer sounding things like civil liberties and human rights?" I asked and received a terse reply. "We sometimes receive shocks of 'devil liberties' at play, resulting in 'human bites from the earth, and all we have done is to have a Holy Vigilance Cell which records such happenings."

To my query if they also used "third degree" methods, the "holycop" cut me short, "No, we believe in strokes." I couldn't follow this and asked the ultimate, "Do you have what they sometimes describe as custodial deaths?"

I was wonderstruck to receive the reply, "No, we have custodial births; anybody dying in your custody gets born up there and his 'account' is recorded by Holy Vigilance." I started feeling shivers down my spine.

Having overcome the shock, I pleaded with him, "But, then, we sometimes do not have enough legal teeth to bite into criminality and...!"

"Shut up, you hypocrite. Have you ever got your quiescent, rather jammed jaws, tested?" the 'holycop' yelled and gave me a gentle upward blow under my chin. Then he opened my jaws and closed them, saying that they had become "functional". Now he sermonised, "What are you going to do with your jammed jaws even if you are given witch-like teeth?"

The "holycop" had put me to enough shame, but I wanted to make the best use of his company to know about celestial policing. I asked him if they too had to do training courses. “Yes, why not? We too have our refreshers”, said he. “These days I am trying to complete a course—Down to Earth”.

When the “holycop” parted company—he had disappeared probably apprehending trouble at the hands of an offended policeman—I found my baton missing.

GANDA MAL

## Ala Bama Coo

The year was 1919. The First World War had just ended counting the scars it left on the wounded globe and its creatures. Mother was there in the verandah of our sprawling bungalow in Agra waiting for my father's return from Berlin. She called out to me, "Ala Bama Coo? Where are you? Know Dad is gonna made Governor on his return!"

With my falling milk teeth, I couldn't then realize what a gubernatorial assignment meant. Even later in life, I couldn't enjoy the privileges reserved for a VIP brat. I could only bask in the reflected glory of my Dad's august office, since I was packed off to Oxford, to return to India with a Bar-at-Law. The year was 1939. Dark clouds of Second World War had begun to blacken the horizon.

Mother had always been overtly fond of Dad plus his rank and epaulets but she often teased him for his playful attitude saying. "You are a kid when out of the uniform." That my Dad could be trusted with the daintiest of tasks and most strategic decisions to be taken, was something my mother would generally take pride in. With mother's coaxing, father had agreed to make India his permanent home.

Parents always had plenty of time for me—their bundle of joy. Having given me a strange name, they would further distort my calling to "Aloo-Bamboo-Coo". Still I loved it till I became conscious and only full of myself.

Having retired as a High Court judge and having been respectfully addressed all through my "sitting" as Mr. Justice AB Coo, I still call to question the wisdom behind my parents in giving me a bizarre name which even when abbreviated, remained equally upsetting – A.B.C. Why was I given a name that sounded more like an ending of a nursery rhyme and a lullaby than a label? It remained my biggest source of angst.

The other day a clerk in my office met me for what he termed was a personal matter. His name was Ganda Mal. The name faithfully sounded its connotations but betrayed this strappingly handsome man's looks. I couldn't help asking him the reason why his parents had named him *Ganda*—the dirty one.

He had a point to make, "Sir, all the eight sons born to my mother before me had died. The priest in our household attributed the tragedies to the effect of an evil eye. When nothing seemed to work the advice of a yokel did. He suggested to my mother to name me 'Ganda Mal' to ward off the ill effect of the evil eye. And so it was, *mai-baap*, that I survived and am standing alive in front of you."

I wrote this story picking up hints on how to write middles by my mentor in journalism late Mr. Ka Naa Subramanyam. Care for what precisely he taught me? Cook up a story of an imaginary past. Add ingredients like high office, octogenarian age-status, a weirdly woven plot and, to cap it all, a grotesque autograph.

Who said only Marlowian and Shakespearean tragedies had the necessary ingredients. Middles too have a discipline of their own.

# Clinking Cacophony

It may sound absurd but England, France and Germany pounded the peace in my humble household and the happiest guy in the entire episode was from Almora. No, it has nothing to do with the two World Wars but the result of my wife's doing an act, which if someone else in the household was found indulging in, was unpardonable.

Here we go clinking. A beautiful crystal in the shape of an apple with a twig and leaf, gifted to my wife by Sir Edward Crew, the Chief Constable of Midlands, U.K., on our visit to that country in 2002, was the first to come crashing. It landed first on the glass table we had purchased as made-to-order for a couple of thousand rupees about a decade-and-half back. Then it touched the floor, breaking into countless pieces, strewn all over as if, for an enhanced effect.

Midway somewhere, it hit the photo frame we got as gift from our hosts in Cergy near Paris, in France. The frame took with it, with a clinking sound a German vase we bought at a duty-free shop for nearly a hundred Euros. Also martyred in the melee were some half a dozen crystals of the shape of a horse, an elephant, a sea-nymph and a peacock we acquired during various trade fairs in Pragati Maidan.

Hearing the rumbling, we all rushed to the drawing room to find a nearly fainting Lady of the House. She did not utter a single word and dumbfounded literally, she looked deep as if through the floor. "What happened? Are you all right? Did you hurt yourself?" were the anxious queries from almost everybody. We accosted her to the bedroom and offered her water.

After a little while she presented herself to be both elucidatory and apologetic. Sweet and consolatory words were showered on her and everyone thanked providence on finding her unhurt, though physically.

She began to settle as also to explain that taking my eldest sister's call informing that she was reaching our place with her grandchildren, to tie me a *rakhi*, she thought it wise to remove all the breakables our of the reach of the naughty ones. "And the 'apple' slipped out of my hands breaking... (sobs)... (more sobs)... everything!" she broke down once again but soon gathered herself.

Seeing her settle down, everyone started exchanging glances with each other. The children left us and made it to the drawing room surreptitiously, one by one. I also followed them only to overhear the titters, "Thank God it was Mamma herself. Or else! Shshsss Papa's here!"

I myself couldn't help but chuckle and sneer. The domestic help from Almora was there collecting the broken pieces and giggling. I am sure he must have set off all the broken glasses and Chinaware, being in our service, for the clinking cacophony blamed on the Lady of the House.

# Chor Bizarre

That Sunday, in order to satisfy an old urge to visit *Chor Bazaar*, I took my driver into confidence, misled the family by telling everyone that I had an important appointment and headed for the place.

I was taking no chances and firmly instructed the driver to remain seated in the car lest it got stolen. Then I stepped out with a surreptitious air. Strange characters sized me up, perceiving me as a potential buyer of their stolen goods, or—heavens forbid—as a thief, myself. I noticed that everybody, regardless of class or stature, operates at the same level here.

A little nervous now, my hand drifted to my purse. It was safely in my pocket, although I had taken the additional precaution of placing no more than a hundred bucks in it. The business of buying and selling was in full swing. Bargaining was obviously a much valued ability. Expressions like "throw away prices" and "sale" fluttered in the air. The only compromise was on warranty. Obviously, no buyer claimed this and no seller stood so committed. What a free trading zone it was! Dubai paled into insignificance.

The range of articles on display was also amazing. You could get anything that could be stolen: Tyres, TVs, CDs, DVDs, monitors, carburetors, bodywear, shoes, seat covers, shades, watches, what not! The brands on offer ranged from *desi* to the most exclusive that Fifth Avenue had to offer. Since I was partial to stationery articles, I found an abundance of them at unbelievably low prices. I purchased a pack of a dozen ballpoint pens for a mere tenner and a roll of brown tape for a fiver. I also purchased a tie for just twenty bucks.

I was beginning to enjoy this outing when a boy sidled up to me and demanded payment for a camera he claimed he had sold to me just a few minutes earlier. I didn't know what to do. Soon a crowd had gathered around us, with everybody exhorting me to pay the "poor" boy his money. I passionately defended myself. I had bought no camera and possessed none, I told them. I even offered to be searched. No one believed me. People soon started to call me names.

The commotion brought a constable on the scene. The matter could be solved only when I took them all to the parking lot and made my driver encounter them. The driver whispered something into the ear of the constable who immediately ordered dispersal.

I even saw the cop winking at the boy who had made those false accusations. Clearly, there was a nexus here but there was no way I could establish it. The driver had evidently told the constable that I was an influential man and that he had better leave me alone.

Back home, my family had a good laugh at my expense. Piped up my younger son with a straight face, “By the way, Papa, did you come across Tagore’s stolen Nobel medallion?” I vowed that I would never visit *Chor Bazaar* again.

Incidentally, the pens had no refills, the brown tape never unwound and the tie lost its colour the moment it was ironed for the first time!

## The Investiture

His Excellency the Governor of Uttaranchal Pradesh, Mr. Sudarshan Agarwal, was then addressing a battery of senior Indian Police Service officers who had graduated in a course held at the ATI, Nainital. He was playing host to these officers at Raj Bhavan.

Neatly decked up in an English suit, he preferred standing against the support of the table in front of him while addressing the officers. His language was lucid and laced with veneer of anecdotes, dwelling in detail about the success stories he came across in life. While exhorting the officers, he chose a mater-of-fact style.

Being the Centre's Observer to this course, I was seated by the side of the Governor. I watched him do some plain talk on the need for the police officers developing a people friendly attitude towards the community at large.

I did not have the faintest of idea that a great and pleasant surprise was in store for me which would thrill me even at its thought, for all the years to come by.

It so transpired that while speaking about the need to ensure peoples' participation in policing, the Governor happened to cite an example that he described was rare to be found. He spoke about a police officer who floated a non-political, non-governmental organisation with nearly a hundred socially conscious citizens of his distinct, some years ago, in a north Indian state. He also recalled the transparency this organisation ensured in police work as also the credibility that the department earned due to this new venture.

He tried to recall the name of the place the officer had been then posted to, but couldn't actually do so, since about a decade had elapsed since when the Governor, as Secretary-General of the Rajya Sabha, first took notice of the officer's initiative. But he was able to recall the name of an adjoining district. This mention of the place rang a bell in my mind.

Somehow I got the impression that the Governor was talking about my district and my own initiative launched with the formation of an NGO—a police-public platform way back in 1998. Modesty held me back but I summoned up courage and stood up, seeking the Governor's attention beseeching: "It was yours truly, Your Excellency!"

"What's your name?" the Governor asked me when I promptly pronounced it. "And what was the name of the place? He queried again. When I gave him the name he repeated it thrice, gazing deep in my eyes fulsomely and with admiration, "Yes! Yes! Yes! So, here you are!"

There was a sparkle of sorts in the eyes of a doting Governor. All eyes got focused on me. The entire gathering was excited at the Governor's "find". And who was me, myself, Elated? Emotional? On cloud nine? Maybe I felt humble, but at the same time I felt several medallions on my chest.

## Do or Dye

Whenever I visit a saloon, I pick an anecdote or two. Here is the latest. It was a "do or dye" situation. Whether to "do" without black hair or "dye" the grey ones!

A man in his 50s with hennaed hair entered and greeted the head barber in a familiar way. He was suitably seated, making me draw a comparison out of envy—only if I was also received in the same manner!

Looking askance in the mirror, since my head had been firmly grabbed by the barber working on my hair, I noticed the goings on, reassured myself that they receive their customers referring to the "equality clause" in the Constitution.

The new customer started chatting with the head-barber. He put his cell-phone on the shelf and asked the "boy" to remind him of it when he was leaving. This confirmed that with age his memory too had begun to fail. Then, when the cloth had been secured around his neck, he "calibrated" his looks deep into the mirror as if he was asking. "When did callowness compound the creases!"

He sought the boy's opinion if it was worth having his moustache dyed as well. Again, I was tempted to look askance. On his upper lips, the man had a broom-like growth with a mix of brown and white strands. I am sure he had tried henna on his moustache, too. My barber once again corrected my posture, while the one attending on the new customer remained noncommittal, and only smiled.

My friend again queried, "At the age of 54, one is bound to have white hair, isn't it? And what's the harm if the natural ageing process is embraced as it comes?" He used the rhetoric this time to fish out a response from the attendant barber, who only hummed lest his master heard him discouraging a customer in not letting his hair dyed and thus lose the charge on labour.

My friend then mentioned Amitabh Bachchan and his white goatee. He went on about Naseeruddin Shah's and Javed Akhtar's original style. But he hastened to add, "But Dilip Kumar dyes his hair even though he is well past the age of 77!"

The head-barber jumped as if he was waiting for an excuse to chip in, "What's the harm in looking younger than your age if you can afford to?" The rise in notation and an unconscious accentuation as he said the sentence clinched the issue. Emboldened, my friend, who was waiting for an argument in his favour, immediately commanded the "boy" to go ahead with dying not only his thatch but his moustache as well.

The naughty head-barber told his assistant with his tongue firmly in cheek, "Apply some dye on this sahib's eyebrows also, otherwise he will feel awkward on being pointed out for not being thoroughly metro sexual." And he turned to the customer saying, "Yes, the in-thing, Sir!"

"Well, it sounds good. After all, you are the one who should be aware of the latest trends in hairstyling. Go ahead! But remind me of my cell-phone when you are done." Having said this, the man turned to the attendant barber the same way I turn to my wife when it comes to "dying" for a cause—to look younger. What else!

## Doting on Balcony

Balcony in a living space is like face on a body. It is the interactive window. It is an overstretched projection and communicates, honestly. It oversees and overhears what is going on not only in the street below but also in the neighbours' households.

Who visits whom? What are the new arrivals in the form of furniture etc. next door? Which neighbour comes at what time? Where from do the marital discord fumes arise and in which house the teenagers return home in the ambrosial hours, fully drunk? Who all in the locality are the balcony-pals, standing and greeting each other, at the same time generating and garnering vibes, and still maintaining their urbane distance! All that and much more.

Balcony, like the *Barsati*, the terrace, a dormer or a window, besides being breathing hole in a building, is a romantic structure too. It gives you not only the leg space but also some fresh air to fill the lungs of your household, howsoever congested.

Sun or rain, breeze or humidity, all by oneself, or, more the merrier, balcony opens up refreshing vistas for felicitating and facilitating a claustrophobic mind. Winters become warm with balcony grabbing as much sunlight, as it can, for you. Come rains and you are there enjoying the cool showers filling you with a thrill of sorts.

If the balcony faces the rising sun or the sea, you are more than rewarded. If it faces the hill, still more benefaction blessed on you. But yes, if the view is docked by some huge building, you have to be content with what Robert Frost, irked at the high risers' dense growth in cities, says in one of his poems...one has to break his neck to see a star.

Balcony is a symbol of concrete liberty. No one takes objection to your standing in the balcony and having a bird's eye view of whatever happens in front of your eyes without inviting frowns from anybody—after all it is your own house and you are not intruding upon anybody else's privacy. More than that you have a right to reap your own balcony blessings.

There are certain things, which are best done only in a balcony, if you want to add real taste to those activities. For example, reading newspaper. Sipping tea. Playing chess, cards or carom. On the holiday one can finish a two-hundred page novel spending the whole day in that cozy and well nestled opening of the house, easily. Or even for idling, the place is highly recommended. If you happen to be a lover of plants, foliage and flowers, balcony spares all space for your pots ensuring enough sunlight and air for them at the same time.

A balcony is a newspaper hawker's delight. He doesn't always have to hit the bull's eye. For a street vendor, the customer is right in his front and within the hearing range which affords him to hold back his shouting, after having an eyeball-to-eyeball contact, thus providing the much desired succor to his vocal chords, at least in your locality. And not the least important is the opportunity available to you if you want to turn your back at the sight of a beggar, in case you are superstitiously skeptical on his curses hurled on you at denial of alms etc.

Balconies have their share of brickbats too. Some high and mighty figures of world fame were targeted here only. Balconies have been known for claiming lives also, giving way under the weight many times. And beware, if you are conservative parents and have Juliets in your house, balconies are accessible to the Romeos, if not for eloping, in the present day scenario of perestroika and glasnost for the generation-X, but at least for stolen kisses. But they are harmless and innocent things and balconies are credited with being home to such basic instincts.

## Did you Do it?

Nosey Parker was snooping around as usual with his beak buried deep in the garbage when to his utter exhilaration he heard the cries in the sky, "Did ye du et—Did ye du et did did?" Mosey Parker looked up to shoot; I mean record in his camera, the exclusive bytes.

The Jungles Babbler, known for his intrusive, naughty and yearn-spinning habits, tweeted at the journo, winked at him and beckoned as if to give the official version. Taken aback, as if someone else had also picked up his exclusive scoop, the journo questioned the impish bird if he also heard the shrieks of, "Did you do it!"

The Babbler knew the anxiety of Nosey Parker and in furtherance of his innate endeavour to tease him he whispered something in the ears of the stringer. "Can you arrange an interview with her? Oh please don't say no!" Well, it happens almost daily. It's not something unusual with her. It's not at all which makes news, I mean the man-biting-the-dog sort of?" the Babbler tried to rubbish the reporting idea.

Nosey Parker insisted, "No dear, what after all was there in Gudiya, Farzana and Anara episodes?

Still we had to drag these poor things out of their homes and present the "real picture" before the people in larger public interest, particularly when every journalist, howsoever incredible, had been doing it."

"Oh yes, there you are. You followed the stories since everyone was (over)doing it. Well, there ees a point in that." The Babbler muffled the "over" part and stressed the "is". Again the tweet of "Did ye du et duet—did did" rented the open skies. Nosey Parker became restless when the Jungle Babbler grimaced turning his eyes away from the curious reporter.

The Babbler asked Nosey Parker to watch and record from a distance when he would be interviewing the victim of "Did you do it?" "*Behenji*, will you tell our audience how do you feel after going through the ordeal of 'Did you do it' since you have been tweeting for quite some time seeking to know the culprit?" The victim squeaked at him scornfully, "D,did ye du et?" "No, no *behenji*, I am a journalist. I don't do myself. I simply fling the others' doing in public-ehm-ehm, bird interest only!" The Babbler again sneered with his tongue firmly in his beak.

Having interviewed the "victim", Nosey Parker rushed and pridefully presented the story to the Editor. Lo and behold, everything got washed out—video, audio and everything. The disgusted Editor gave good amount of birdshit to Nosey Parker who rushed back to look up the Jungle Babbler.

He overheard the naughty Babbler talking to the forgetful Lap Wing: "I knew that you as habit would forget the place of your laying eggs and then scream around as if someone had stolen them squeaking 'Did you do it', but this Nosey Parker fellow thought he had picked up the best of scoops."

Having known this now, Nosey Parker asked them as if cheated, "But what happened to my recording?" Replied the Jungle Babbler, "Don't you know we have beepers and jammers planted under our wings to ward off the recording done by the likes of you in larger bird interests." They laughed to their guts content while Nosey Parker again buried his beak in the garbage.

## Withdrawal Symptoms

Yes, consciously or otherwise, one does feel the withdrawal symptoms in the New Year. These may be of different kinds with different people. Yet, a feeling of correcting some wrong, of which one is habitual for the past some time, takes the better of him, not only in his actions but the thinking process as well.

Most people would continue to write the date as if it belonged to the year gone by. And then with some effort they'd amend it, reassuring themselves of the continuum of existence in the New Year. The correction thus made confirms the hangover of the year that rolled into eternity, never to return.

The withdrawal syndrome fills one with a sense of loss in so far as the diaries and calendars are concerned. But this loss is compensated in acquisition of the new ones with uncrumpled and crisp pages with unruffled folds. The contents of the old diaries may still have nostalgic notes stored for posterity but the promise that the blank slots hold balances the psychological depravity.

The most obsolete thing and rightly to be treated as such should be the "year's holiday-list". I personally am thrilled to have a new one. And since the indolence and lethargy that had been squeezed out to the exuberance of this old list, it deserves to be filled with some alternate and refreshing replenishment. A new holiday-list is the panacea to ward off gone-year withdrawal symptoms found mostly in the Indian *babudom.*

The emotional fools make New Year resolutions to stand by, but in many cases they do not live up to their commitments and promises made to themselves since if they were so strong-willed, they wouldn't wait for the turn of the year for effecting their resolve. They feel the gone year withdrawal symptoms more than anyone else. This is so, also because, mostly the New Year resolutions are on giving up vices and less on acquiring virtues.

Well, the business types would do stocktaking exactly when the old year-ends and new one begins for they generally had had some deity or the other's blessing for a fixed duration. The fortunetellers also guide the "stars" of their destiny in an already announced time slot. They too need some counseling to overcome to gone year withdrawal symptoms.

Call me mad, or even selfish, but this year I have decided on an altogether different way to come out of the gone year withdrawal symptoms and keep feeling elated when friends would call for nearly a week at least to greet and Happy New Year to me. Want to know it? Well, I will not say and thus share; and thus exhaust or empty, my own good wishes but will only receive them for their therapeutic properties. Thank you friends!

## Queer Thoughts

How should this bearded man look like after a shave? How about this man without the moustaches he has? What kind of patches are there on the face of this pink-painted blonde? How would this wrinkled, old hag have looked in the prime of her youth? Doesn't this person, who otherwise normally wears spectacles, look entirely a different being without them, or with contact lenses fitted behind the eye-lashes? How would this beautiful and stunning dame look like when she becomes *Dadi Amma*?

All these and many more inquisitive queries keep troubling me occasionally. But, honestly (!), this tendency has nothing to do with harbouring a desire to have see-through-clothe goggles. Otherwise why should everybody be exclaiming, "*Choli ke peeche Kyaa hai*!" You know how a Haryanvi old woman reacted to this. She said "*Re haad sain, haad*" (O' brat it's bones, bones and nothing else!).

Once I went to attend a function in a school for the blind. Excepting about half a dozen of us blessed with eyes, the rest had never seen the light. They welcomed us, sang for us, and delivered speeches with full confidence. But when they all expressed the desire to have a group photo, the queer-thoughts cell in my brain got activated.

"After receiving the photograph, how should they all be in a position to experience the feeling one has, looking at one's photograph, with no light in the eyes?" I thought. I was reminded of John Milton: "They also serve who stand and wait." But, surely, standing and waiting is totally different from experiencing queer feelings.

Another strange feeling that I often experience is a craving to see how I look like while asleep! In my childhood, I remember trying to close my eyes and seeing through the "cracks" of the eye-lashes into a mirror. But never, ever, could I know for myself the way I wanted to be seen. Even in my dreams I could not see how I looked—obviously—but what to do with queer thoughts?

A friend suggested, "Why don't you get yourself photographed while asleep!" "No, no, it presents a horrible picture, as if you are dead," I said. But my friend quoted a beautiful couplet: "*Palak se palak mili aur neend meethee aa gayee; Kya yahi thee wo maut jisse umar bhar darte rahe.*" (Coming together of the eye-lashes lulled me into deep sleep; was it really this kind of sleep induced death which dreaded me all through the life?).

Well, thoughts may be queer, but there is definitely an element of life in them. They may be twisted, but they reflect the facts of life.

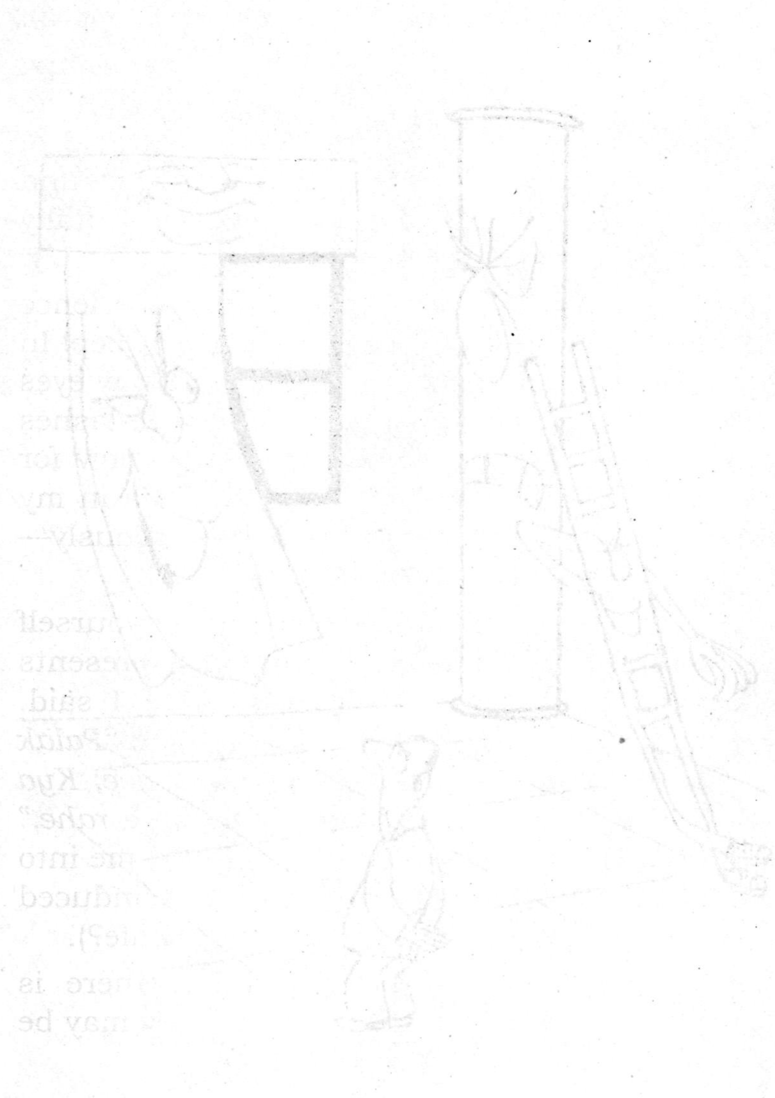

## A House Divided

Wading through the aisles in a castle, I witnessed a tumultuous scene. I hid behind a column and heard the goings-on. Good Lord! Do the structures too suffer from a superiority complex and air their assertions of self importance, deep-rooted in their stone-psychology?

The raised pulpit was in audience to the deliberations. Pinnacles were clamouring their claim on arches, cloisters, and even roofs. "Our pointed ends, aiming high, surge above all but while getting pulled down, why should we be the only targets?"

An arch (rival) sneered and silenced the pinnacles, "It's because of your soaring ambition, my Dears. Don't you remember Icarus, with wax wings, nearing the Sun, falling flat, down to earth?"

The windows whispered to each other and put forward their claim, "We allow views not only from the inside, but also from outside, and thus facilitate transparency. We initiate communion without porous casements to make marriages of convenience, or elope sometimes, to make strange bedfellows."

The ladder in a corner, chuckled and whispered in the ears of the pelmets, "Why do they need curtains then?" Windows eves dropping on the ladder, retaliated, "Gone are the days of glass-houses." The parapets chimed in for the windows, "We, too, have embrasures to allow guns being fired from, then why blame only the curtains? An opening, after all, is an opening."

An announcement from the pulpit reminded everyone that scandalous, thorny and intricate issues belonging to lobbies, balconies, corridors etc. needed immediate attention of the house, and any reference to foreigners should be avoided. While in India behave like the Indian structures do.

The walls which had remained silent then seconded the reminder from the pulpit and asked the lobby to come forward. "The main issue with us, the lobbies, today is that whatever transpires here gets passed on to the fourth estate via the corridors even as a powerful claim is made of maintaining secrecy," said the lobby.

On a point of personal explanation, the corridors said that they too shared walls and could not avoid sharing information which gets resounded.

Now it was the turn of the roof, admitting vicarious responsibility, to take affront to these remarks. "Well, we too share many things with almost everybody here. And we are, you will kindly acknowledge, above you. Don't we, too, collapse sometimes with all that burden and our own weight? We wonder what would happen if supporters like walls, pillars, columns, arches etc. were not there? Even Robert Frost wondered—

Something there is that does not love a wall; it brings it down." Is it not, swearing by our common minimum, cemented programme, our duty to let the edifice not fall!

The balcony, from a vantage point, looking askance at the watch towers through the windows, appreciated the plight of the roof and took to task the lobbies and the corridors for their belligerent postures, irresponsible utterances, scheming tendencies, and forging alliances.

The altar looked upward and scoffed at the balcony, "From there, you can only make tall claims blowing to winds the reality that genetically you hang in balance and it is only us who get trampled with heavy boots and nimble feet, alike. You can only find fault with others."

From a quaint corner, the stairs stared at the balcony and altar, to remind if 'stairs' was not the 'case', both balcony and altar would not have been able to reach each other.

The pillar I was leaning on proved to be a stumbling block and gave way, shouting in apprehension, "Who's there?" And before I could gather myself I was cornered from all sides: "Who's he? What is he doing here?" I wanted to flee through a window, but a curtain held me back.

I frowned at the curtain and to hit a bargain I reminded him of "behind the curtain scenes."

A bat flapped its wings and cautioned the traders in the adjoining horse-stable: "Aey, he is an innocuous one, a creative writer to be precise, known to be building castles in the air. But beware, he may tell the world the secrets of the house!"

The stones fell silent, while the echoes still rippled in the air. And a poor me, an average Indian voter, found myself again in suspended animation.

## Of Shaking Earth and Souls in Slumber

Having landed in the metropolis called the Babus' Dilli from my home state about six months back, I had been longing to befriend or at least know each and every person who I was sharing my roof, floor, walls, stairs, corridors, travel-car lifts, etc. etc.

I wished to acquaint myself with the people I have been living with but they could only be seen shut up in their closets, soon after their appearance in the doors and windows once in a while, quite bereft of all interactions, exchange of gestures of human coexistence, discharge of the humane emotions and feelings.

Diwali came, Christmas came, Id came and came the New Year Eve but we the residents of the Pragati Vihar Hostel, in the heart of the country's capital, never saw, nay, knew each other, save for one fine morning till the building that housed us all, shook and shattered driving us out of our "cells" exclaiming, enquiring confirming, announcing— "An earthquake.....!?" It was only afterwards that we came to know that the earthquake fury was disastrous in a part of our country.

Living in the cemented structures, even during a very short stay, I had witnessed no commenting of our social ties and no ice breaking, when, thanks to the seismological shaking at least we behaved the way human beings are excepted to behave, may be in distress only.

As we were preparing ourselves to watch the Republic Day Parade on the television, I felt as if the bed was swinging. I looked towards my wife who, ignorant of the earthquake, was stirring sugar in her cup of tea. For once, I thought it was due to the stirring that the bed was shaking but no, even the fan, who no "provocation" during the ensuing winters and as if a pigeon had just flown from it appeared to be oscillating very leisurely.

"It could only be an earthquake," I shouted a la the sailor who noticed the iceberg in Titanic and headed towards the balcony. One by one the doors and windows of our adjoining flats in all blocks started opening with the inmates looking apprehensive and alarmed but still needing to confirm before they finally set out for safe open space. From a distance each one of us sought information through glances only. Such a scene had never taken place during the recent past.

I shouted to wife: "It's an earthquake, darling!" and she summoned me to the room to be near her as if I could stop even the earthquake from taking place as I am notorious for taking good care of the house quakes, if that be the right coinage. She could hardly slip into her sneakers when we moved out to join the train of the panicked men, women and children; some excited, some frightened, some invoking Gods and I, remembering my children.

"Why the hell, after all, they preferred to have a night out yesterday only, at a friend's place.

We climbed down the stairs. I signalled to some others using the cable cars to avoid them. Out in the open, we were all talking to each other for a change. Sharing experiences. What did each one of us feel on the first swing? How was it confirmed? There were grim faces. There were the glowing ones too hiding their fears insidiously. There was apprehension, another manifestation of the fear of metaphysical, supernatural and the unknown. Those already out in the open did not notice what had happened and were bewildered to see an unusual sight of all the residents being outdoors, at one time. At a time, when we all feared for our existence. At a time when egos, inhibitions, complexes, resolve to make room for fellow feeling among the human beings.

"The earthquake which hit and very badly at that the Bhuj region and killed unknown number of people, gave us mild tremors in Delhi, to shake us out of our steel frames into being with our fellow homosapiens, but why it always be so, that being co-sufferers of a near-catastrophic predicament only that it should remind us of our being the species who are naturefed with the milk of human kindness?" was the question I was asking myself while climbing the stairs to reach back my apartment. Yes, apart-meant!

## Dead Handshakes

Unconsciously, sometimes one imagines things unthinkable. But, it is really hilarious if the impossible gets translated into something real, happening very much before your eyes.

Have you ever felt the persons in photographs coming out of the frames and shaking hands with you? Have you seen them talking and even walking with you?

I came across a teacher of English who is capable of bringing persons alive out of the pictures and initiating a dialogue with them.

We were conversing in his study where there was a beautiful scenery put on the wall. It depicted a brook gurgling past hard-to-move stones. In the backdrop were hills, trees, wild ferns and moss.

I pointed out to my friend, "Well, I have the capability to perch myself on that tall Deodar's leafy tendrils and hang about them at the same time enjoying not only the swing but literally a bird's-eye view of the entire scene down below."

He smiled mysteriously as if trying to conceal something from me and as if he had a wonderful capability to disclose up his sleeves. But he kept quiet.

Having noticed this challenge, I went on, "You see that small wooden bridge on the rivulet (we are talking about the picture itself); I can walk over it. And going a little further on that lagoon, with my pants pulled up to the knees, crossing the cold water, I can rest there for hours and hours basking in the Sun without being bound by time and space."

I continued with what must have sounded like a boast, "Well, I can do fishing with the angler's hat on my head in those shallow waters of the spill, accumulated in that made-to-measure lake on the side of the rivulet."

Now my friend confuted me, smiling and bearing my reverie, enough being enough, "Can you eat those fish and...!" I stopped in my pictorial escapade and was grounded, dashed-down in my delightful fancy. He had something more interesting to tell and I looked agape at him.

"You know the dead appearing in obituary columns of newspapers!" I still remained bereft of speech, when he began "I see those dead person in pure flesh and blood appearing to me not like apparitions, but as acquaintances."

He continued, "Smiling, they tell me about the life they lived; time they spent, enjoying or otherwise; their well-wishers, friends and foes; their investment in things humane; their being cheated or rewarded; their relationship with the family members who, after their demise, tried to immortalise them with sweet remembrances and so on."

I was amazed at this man's flights of fancy and the tenacious ability to bring the dead alive, giving me an inferiority complex, for he had by then proved that he was a cut above me and innumerable romanticists.

Then I asked my friend the silliest question: "Do these dead conjure up from the pictures in the obituary columns, and inform you of how they died?"

"No, by then they are dead", he said. My friend knows where the fanciful flights face the rock-realities of life.

## Embarrassing Encounters

You must have often encountered situations when someone asked you if you recognized him or her. And with a vigorous mental gymnastics, if you were not able to place this person, your reactions could have been numerous. For example, "Oh, yes, do you think I can forget you like that"! "Okay, if you will not recognize me being a big man, shall I do the same to you"; "*kamaal hai, aap bhi bhoolne wali cheese hain*?"

All these expressions bring a strange but readable expression on your face since your sheepish countenance becomes so transparent that you yourself feel embarrassed. And imagine if the person not rightly recognized shoots up, saying, "Okay, tell me who am I?" You are gone then.

Some people are good at remembering names and others at remembering faces and still others have both these qualities. But there are those, too, who are not really slow-witted but fail to respond to their recognizing stimuli even if they are stirred with so many references—"Didn't we meet at Mr. Gupta's party?"! "Didn't I call upon you with Mr. Sharma?"; "God forbid, if someone tells before your wife that he had met you when you were with Miss so and so!"

A factor which cannot be ignored is that certain people have similar faces or gait or stature or even a hair-style that betrays your recognizing faculties to have a full play and afford you proper identification. Another situation is when you will only wait for the other person to speak out and then only you are able to tell him or her who he or she is. But a mischievous smile flashed against your grinning teeth makes matters worse, and the other party understands that you have not really understood.

I remember a friend who confessed that he made advances to a pretty woman traveling in Shatabdi Express from Chandigarh to Delhi, though, "communication" was limited to exchanging glances and staring only, without any dialogue ensuing in the deal.

When they alighted from the train, the woman walked ahead while my friend trailed (or chased?). And the inevitable happened. A very close relative of this man was there on the platform to receive his wife, the lady in question. When the two were introduced by the relative, my friend blushed while the woman with a winsome glee in her eyes joined her husband, saying, "Yes, I know he is Mr....!"

Sometimes, as it comes suddenly from the blue and one is not able to muster up one's faculties of recollection of names and faces with a conscious effort, there always exists a thought block, which is the root cause for the suffered embarrassment.

And it once happened with me. I was sitting in my office when a seemingly very familiar man came in. I welcomed him greeting, “Come, Mr. Sharma, come!” And, suddenly, I realized he might not be Mr. Sharma. But I made good my mistake and, in an obvious bid to assuage his (hurt) feelings, I offered him a seat with a, now corrected version of his calling, “Please sit down, Mr. Shashi Kant”. He obliged me by smiling. We had a good chat, but all through I was feeling guilty of not having recognized the man properly.

He took leave me, and I called out for the office attendant. Out of curiosity as also to confirm if I was right—since this name was a frequent visitor to my office—I asked the attendant, “Do you know who he was?”

“Why, Sir, don’t you know?” he said. “He was Mr. Shashi Kant Sharma!”

## Wife's Conscience-Keeper on *Karwa Chauth*

It was my wife's "silver jubilee" *Karwa Chauth*. Twenty-five years may be eternity for the rest of the world, but for the two of us it was as if we had been blessed with conjugal bliss only yesterday (excluding the courtship period, of course!). In all these years, I had not changed even a bit about my typically Indian "husbandry".

The day began with instructions to the domestic help. The do's and dont's were notified in clear terms. Nothing was to be served in two portions. Not even water, for the boy might out of habit bring two glasses and my wife might drink a little by mistake and thereby commit an "indiscretion". "*Khana sirf sahib ke liye banega*," my wife too joined to say in a matter-of-fact manner.

During the early phase of our married life, my wife used to coax me into observing a fast with her: "All good husbands are supposed to stand by their spouses in difficult times." But being a hard-nut, I maintained my expected standards of masculinity, guided more by the time-tested traits of playing husband than mutual feeling. After all, I had to think about what society could say—I dreaded being called hen-pecked, one who swears by the wife!

The day of *Karwa Chauth* being a holiday, I followed my wife to all the nooks and corners of the house, particularly to the kitchen, lest she be led to consuming any edible stuff. I doubled as her conscience-keeper, doubtless adding to her woes. The fact she told me that, for the last one quarter-of-a-century, she had been taking care of herself, did not cut much ice.

I watched her dress in a green silk saree we had purchased for the occasion. I noticed her tenderly putting on bangles on the wrist. I saw her putting a bindi with extra care in the middle of the forehead. And I nearly felt butterflies in my stomach when I put sindoor on her head as she touched my feet. Rather than giving in to the intensity of my feelings, I chose to think I was the best "husband" in the world and that my wife was still the prettiest woman on earth—my *zohra-jabeen.*

By afternoon some ladies came to our house to listen to the *kahani* which a Brahmin woman was supposed to relate to the fasting women. I eaves-dropped and listened to the story, the plot of which would frighten any husband-loving Hindu-wife. I, for once, thought that the theory of imitation propounded by Aristotle had its universal relevance. Quietly I went to the kitchen and prepared tea for my wife. The domestic help couldn't help giggling, for he had never seen me look at kitchen even by mistake, let alone enter it.

The evening set in, and I escorted my wife to the rooftop to "discover the moon". After all it was the moon's turn now to clinch the issue of breaking the fast. I tried to locate the celestial body with sincerity. Lo and behold, the shining ball appeared on the northeastern horizon to relieve countless souls. Who said I didn't take care of my better three-fourth as they say these days on *Karva Chauth*? And, if I said at the beginning that the husband in me hadn't changed a bit over the past several years, well, I was lying.

# I in You

I marvel at some people's clairvoyance in entreating others while reserving their own share of prize-niceties. Very often we experience being felicitated but the contribution of the person thus extending courtesies gets recognised, as if by default. They employ a catch in the deal very tactfully.

The one who is on the wrong side of 60, and who pens and recites a *sehra*, fishes out an invitation for himself to sing another one, when the son of the soon-to-wed bridegroom would tie himself in the nuptials, may be 25 years later. But his gesture is well-taken. His "pound of flesh" is doubly assured by the hoi polloi. In the deal he seeks a bonus to live even beyond that quarter of a century!

Our family priests knew that I was the only son in the household, a fact that had all through been emotionally exploited by them while forecasting events relating to me, when they interacted with my mother. They took care not to say offending things curtly—rather, the warnings were clothed in sober semantics.

"The boy may spend a couple of months convalescing in a hospital in the month of *phagun*!" they would prophesy. Apprehensive and solicitous, mother would ask for a remedy. "Make charity on *poornamasi* to Brahmins and it will take care of the 'event'. Today is the propitious day and we your *purohits*, but the grace of the Almighty, are available!" the priests proffered. I remember them carrying loads of wheat or rice with them. That I got my hand fractured but as late as by five years is another matter.

In the villages in Haryana, till recently, if a new bride touched the feet of elderly women, the latter were expected to say their blessings by word of mouth. Sample: *Boodh suhagan ho! Bhai jeeyen, Saain jeeye! Beta de Bhagwan*! (May your husband live till your old age. May your brothers and caretaker live long. May you be blessed with a son).

Meaning thereby that although there was no blessing ascribed to the poor woman directly but in blessing her with related "benedictions", male chauvinism was reinforced by none other than the women themselves. Was this imploring done for seeking social and physical security in all-male world of Haryana? The mythological tale of Satyawan and Savitri is a case in point. Savitri invokes Yama on the death of her husband Satyawan, on the strength of her fidelity, purity, fortitude and righteousness.

Happily convinced, Yama grants her a wish when she asks for 100 sons. "*Tathaastoo*!" And the wish was granted. Then Savitri beseeches Yama to bring her dead husband to life, which was not the deal, but for whose life she could never dream of becoming mother of 100 sons. Yama had to concede since the divine ordainment was not like a routine office order that could be rescinded.

A modern-day clerk would have been fired for not being able to notice the catch in the projected wish. The fact remains that in seeking and greeting we do not efface ourselves completely. But how cleverly the presentation is made, is the key to employ a catch.

## The Coast Guard

Verily the wise say: "Police are neither good for friendship, nor are they to be taken on as enemies; they spare none. Not even their own bloodline in khaki." Highly motivated and conscientious of their breed, this "cult" needs most desirably to be kept at an arm's length.

Such was the impression gathered by a small-framed colleague of mine who hadn't lost his boyish looks as yet, despite the Haryana Police's best efforts to boot, his first ever honey-moon, at that farthest tip in the Indian Ocean, called Kanyakumari.

Well, with the newly acquired marital wisdom, they decided to have a long walk along the beach, with the seas being in a turbulent mood. Every time a near-tidal wave lashed shorewards, to lap up all in the way, they would curl themselves up, near being jelled and in thus being so glued to each other, they experienced a closeness of sorts, which the coming days of staying in cohabitation, might rob them of, as it generally happens.

But those were the moments they could savour, for all their lifetime, to be reminded or, while trying to resolve disputes experienced later in life. Little did they realize then, that something more furious than the leaping waves, was going to come their way, that could land them in police custody.

The couple made themselves comfortable on the manmade shorewall and were busy exchanging sweet nothings when, facing the shore, the better-half looked at a constable approaching them with a large baton, almost charging and threatening. Shocked, the wife murmured the arrival of the menacing apparition.

"Hey, who are you two? And what do you think are you doing here? Where have you come from—you seem to have eloped, as is usual with the spoilt generation of today!" the cop hurled a volley of interrogative adjectivals attributable to the unsuspecting couple, who almost separated physically.

"Well, Sir, we are responsible people," pleaded my friend, enlightening the cop that they were a duly and legally married couple.

Not convinced, the cop fired another salvo: "Have you seen your face in the mirror, you brat? Have you really grown up to take this woman in what you call a marriage? Your baby face defies your argument and so does your skimpy, scanty, velvety and feathery hairline on your upper lip!" thundered the uniformed man, ordering them to follow him to the police station.

Of course, all this while my friend's wife remained quiet, blushing while he himself was virtually at sea, to make his persecutor believe him. At the same time he was trying to recover from the shock of being perceived and commented upon, as not really grown-up for marriage. But then, by now, enough was enough, and since what the cop intended doing next was to drag the couple to his already declared safe haven, my friend disclosed his identity.

To put a real stamp on his assertion and announcement as a senior police officer, he went on to tell the constable that the district superintendent was his batch-mate.

Taken aback, the man turned white, pleading: “Can’t help it. Sir, just a day back a couple committed suicide here and my SHO took me to task for not being able to prevent it!”

While the incident ended on a happy note with the beat policeman tendering profuse apologies, our couple grinned away to glory.

# Seasonal Favours

Having become wiser due to an occurrence that took place about a year back, I did not approach the authorities for a seasonal favour this winter, despite its bone-chilling intensity.

It so happened that in January last, I filed a formal request with the officials concerned with pruning and maintenance of flora, since tall eucalyptus trees blocked the sun on my roof which largely remained in shade that was cool enough to kill, with even the slightest stirring of breeze, if you happened to be there.

One full month rolled over when I thought it prudent to remind the department concerned since *sarkari* people attach much importance to a booster-catalyst in the form of a reminder. Nothing moved till I turned the February leaf on the calendar. I shot off another reminder followed by a telephone pleading, in a mild and meeky pitch after the fashion of the beggars near Sai Mandir on the Lodhi Road.

My efforts paid dividends when at noontime, when I had come home for lunch, an overseer ably attended by a foreman of the horticulture department visited our roof, for what they called a spot inspection (normally the cops indulge in that game very often). Convinced they went back with a promise that prompt action would follow. Nothing happened even during the month of March.

The All Fools' Day last year was quite warm when I received a call from my father. He asked us to join him for Baisakhi celebrations since we couldn't visit the village on Holi that season. We spent about a fortnight with father, going for a stroll in the fields and bathing almost daily twice a day in the cold water in the nearby canal to beat the heat of April.

After attending the Baisakhi festival around the middle of Eliot's "cruelest month" and having seen the wheat ripen, on my lands back home, we came back to Delhi, only to find the surprise that was in store for us.

There were about half a dozen men, like the *vanarsainiks* of Lord Hanuman in Ashok Vatika where Sitaji was held captive, atop the eucalyptus trees, with axes, saws and halberds, performing a very neat and clinical job of chopping the branches that extended like our neighbourly country Pakistan's ever soliciting loan-arm to the US, to my roof. These were to provide me with the much needed cool shade when, I thought, I would sit in the mornings, sipping tea from my cuppa and enjoy reading the newspapers.

"Hey! You fellas! Stop that" I barked at those who were responsible for not only robbing me of my sunshine during the winters but were hell-bent on depriving, me of my cool shade in the ensuing summers as well, but to no avail. When I took up the issue with the leader of the gang and told him that pruning was not required anymore then, he quipped: “But you are supposed to inform us in time, sir!”

“Do they collect their salary of the month six months later than when it becomes due?” I kept wondering and grumbling with four-letter words coming to my mind in gay abundance. I felt like someone whose molar was extricated when the dentist was supposed to take the canine tooth out.

## Flowery Epaulets

On my posting to a district, I met Babu Lal who was "detailed" for attending on me and was to be my favourite throughout the years to come by. There wasn't anything extraordinary about this man but he, it was said, enjoyed the confidence of over a dozen of my predecessors. He was a head-constable but never donned his uniform.

Within a few days of our association, I discovered that Babu Lal wasn't as meek and submissive as he showed himself to be. He, in fact, was a big bully who could make even the hardest nut of a thanedar to shake in his pants, only by informing him about sahib bahadur's displeasure of the man who possessed an ambidextrous sleight of hand in accepting—you know what I mean.

Well, "pleasure or otherwise" of the senior officers is capable of making even those who hold presidential and gubernatorial positions go green with envy. Babu Lal knew this and understood its implications well. I heard him speak too little. And smile? It would cost him a hundred worlds.

One day, Babu Lal was reclining on a chair with his made a couple of bougainvillea petals rest on the flap. It was then that I called out for him. I asked for a packet of cigarettes and was about to point out the pink petals stuck on the folds of his white cap but held back, since I myself was amused at the sight.

Generally, Babu Lal kept a packet with him to immediately pass on to me on demand but that day he failed. Disturbed by this a bit, he hurriedly pulled out his bicycle. On his way out, the sentry on the gate threw a mischievous smile at him, tittering: “Babu Lalji aaj to bade phool-wool saja rakhe hain!”

In police parlance the shoulders or epaulets are indicative of one’s rank. But, Babu Lal missed both, the point and the pun, and giving the sentry a stern look, peddled his way to the paanwala around the corner.

The vendor at the paan shop, squishing the betel leaf juice in his mouth, made a tickling dig at Babu Lal repeating the sentry’s remarks verbatim. My assistant again dismissed the felicitation and sniggered at the paanwala while collecting the cigarette pack, unmindful of the attributes to the petals that were adorning his cap.

When he confronted me I couldn’t help smiling at him then and saying: “Ye phool abhi tak laga rakhey hain!” Babu Lal couldn’t afford to take me lightly. He was taken aback realizing something unusual was happening with him that day. It was only when I referred with a pointed finger to the petals that the point was driven home—of his flaunting the “flowery medallions”.

I saw a sheepish Babu Lal smile only once, and for all times to come. I came to know about his encounters with the sentry and the paanwala only when Babu Lal himself told the entire episode to my steno.

# Airport in the Bedroom

Mobility is the guiding spirit behind all development. Be static and you are finished. A light-house, thus, may help steer ships to desired destinations, yet it is devoid of the driving force.

Speed and sensation have a common bloodline, just as cars and racing do. But I, for one, am not at all impressed with the latest cars which lack all the 'drive' in the sense that there are automatic, and with computerised controls of speed, negotiations, movements and halting.

You can read newspapers, shave, sip coffee and become a stone on the wheel (?).

Mobility and modernity go hand in hand. The stars traverse their ordained path, yet seem to the human eye grounded in the sky...until a part(icle) breaks up and flashes down at mankind. Yet with modern sky-scrappers, laments Robert Frost, in one of his poems, one had to almost break ones neck and throw it out of a window, "to see a star".

This reminds us of the triviality of the human self...even as it tells us of the magnanimity of the human mind, which keeps exploring, path-finding, and to coin new expressions—mooning, marsing and even sunning. The fate of Icarus, who as the legend goes, flew too close to the Sun, got his wings seared and was hurled down, has in no way deterred the modern day "space-seeking scientists".

A bureaucrat friend of mine adds a philosophical dimension to this vast expanse of all that exists and all that appears to exist. He says that whenever he feels he is becoming too big for his boots, he goes to the rooftop at night, and takes a good look at the starry expanse.

It makes him realise and appreciate his smallness, his nothingness...and perhaps also his uselessness. And he returns to his room a wise man—just another human being.

But how many of us think that way!

Confucius said, "I hear, I forget, I see, I remember, I do, I understand." Let me imagine myself in a cockpit. There are innumerable operations to be understood...and performed. There are countless buttons to be pressed and released. I press a button and see what happens.

I am landing, I hear many beeps and clicks. Many glows and flashes appear. I am grounded in my bedroom. All around me are little bulbs glowing and beaming from the TV, the VCR, the wall clock, the red-eyed switch control of the cooler, the fluorescent tube and the transformer.

I want to sleep motionless and undisturbed—be static, so to say—but there are these illumined and blinking run(a)ways all around me. It is here in the modern era that speed and sleep have an interface. Sleep, one can, but only in dreams... with click-click lullabies and flash-flash glows.

## Yes, Darling! No, Darling!

All colourful beauties they were there. From ultra-mods to old hags; from the best maintained to the yesteryear's heart throbs' from the fast moving to the (now) wriggling ones; from those driving to the driven. Yes, I am talking of cars of VVIPs at a party get-together.

But the most noticeable thing about them was their assuming of airs. These darlings of men who mattered reflected the status of those who they carried. They had a certain aura around them; a faithful reflection of their paramours' stature which was proclaimed to the cops on duty by their chauffeurs. Yes, I am talking of the cars.

What is beside the point is the cops' ordeal in handling these keeps of the men at the helm of affairs. Well, they were there emblazoned—blood red, not-so-sober white, apparently pale, bottle green, royal blue, silver-coated, gold-plated, crimson, violet, grey and so on. The faded ones had less aggressive chauffeurs, naturally. Yes, I am talking about cars.

From the parking place to the boarding podium they steered in a bid to rush ahead of all anxious to lift and secure their riders. When these darlings of VVIP's had an eyeball-to-eyeball contact with their respective men in the waiting, none could command them to move. Not even the traffic cop. Yes, I am talking about cars.

The chauffeur thundered when he saw the traffic cop "...Sahib ki gari hai!"

The poor cop grumbled, "All these vehicles belong to some important Sahib or the other".

And the cop too, true to his training, kept whistling at these darlings of the Sahibs. Yes, I am talking about cars.

The dilatory boarding was whipped up when a senior darling continued the blaring of horn from behind. And here was the question of party discipline. The podium beauty moved with her riders to give way to her follower. Yes, I am talking about cars.

Well, they were beaming. They were driving roughshod over other's bonnet-shoulders. There were growling. There were the inviting types. There were the outshining ones. There were cute, shapely, bitchy and hot. All steered clear their way trying to overtake others. No, I am not talking about cars.

# Man, Moment and Millennium

How important should be the moment which will tick the old millennium off, out of its existence by kicking right near the cusp and bring the new one to its being. How crucial should be that moment which will quietly roll into eternity and herald a new beginning. How singled out would be that moment which both millennia would claim to be their own. "Oh to be equal in status to that moment!" many may cherish.

Moment after moment, minute after minute, hours after hours, day after day, month after month, year after year, decade after decade, century after century, and likewise such a moment takes shape and fades out. And so will that special, that unique, that different moment, take birth and make history.

History of its being. History of its end. History of its importance. History of its relevance. And History of its nothingness. Could a man be likened to a moment?

Countless people would feel their existence quite differently in the 21st century. Others may not even know of the change. Still others may find in that situation as if nothing moves except nothingness.

At the same time there would be innumerable people who would enjoy every bit of that precious moment. Its beginning, its being and its end. Isn't it surprising to be dwelling so much on one moment? One single moment? One special moment? One moment like other moments? Just another moment!

Then why so much anxiety? Why so much curiosity? Why so much of wait? Why so much of concern? Why so much of so much?—for a mere moment: I never knew that a moment was such a complex entity.

Surely then, moment can definitely be likened to a man. Moment and man in their glory. Moment and man in their being. Movement and man in their spacing, where space does not exist at all. All the more, moment can be "felt" like man.

But hang on. I have a visual right in front of me purely in bones and flesh. I see the merry-makers. I see those rejoicing. Some drowned in drunkenness. Others sun in spirits. Still others frolicking in frenzy and euphoria. One fellow sleep-walks trampling, the other sleeping on a walking path of the metropolis roadside. "Hay, wake up! Scoundrel! New millennium has arrived! It is the turn of the century." He barks.

"The scoundrel" wakes up not really agitated, takes a turn to the other side (like a century) and sleeps on. The moment has come and gone. The man has woken up turned and slept again. The millennium has arrived and will end soon. Yes, very "soon"!

Moment after moment. Tick after tick. Pulse after pulse. Well, tick and pulse can be likened.

So can be moment and man. Tick enlivens up and consumes the moment; pulse enlivens up and consumes the man. Welcome Millennium—ticking, pulsating and consuming.

## The Enigmatic Driver

Two boys hijacked my peace of mind for nearly an hour in a barber saloon recently. Sandwiched between Rahul and Nitin, my haircut began with the clip-clap of the scissors, amid a tete-a-tete of the two cronies. This is how it all went...

Rahul said he was disturbed by loud music played on a car stereo as early as at six in the morning. “Was it a white car?” asked Nitin “Yes” Rahul replied. “With registration mark 1069?” queried Nitin. “Yes, something like that!” Rahul confirmed. “Oh Yaar! It could be none else but my idiot car-driver,” said Nitin.

Rahul again said: “So boring yaar, almost at the dead of night he was listening to Mata Ki Bhenten and very lousy ones. None was based on least film tunes” Nitin confirmed: “Then surely it was my driver. Good-for-nothing fellow!”

“Do you know what happened to the cricket match?” Nitin changed the topic. Rahul said with a genuine sense of loss, “No yaar! The morning cacophony disturbed me so much that it slipped out of my head.” “O.K.! Was this man a lean one and bent a little?” Nitin asked again referring to the driver. “Yes” Rahul confirmed. “Oh yaar, it can be nobody else than my lowly car-driver!" said Nitin.

"How was your visit to the Auto-Expo?" Nitin again digressed. "Disgusting. I was expecting something like a Sachin Ferrari being there for a free-ride." Replied Rahul when Nitin sought afresh: "Did the fellow listening to the devotional songs wear a brown jacket?" Rahul hummed in the affirmative. "I can have a bet now; this unscrupulous fellow was certainly my car-driver," declared Nitin.

I began to lose my cool. Even the barber pointed out perspiration on my forehead. I told him not to mind it since I was a bit hyper-tensive. But I had decided in my heart of hearts that if the boys continued with their prattle and the enigmatic car-driver anymore, I wouldn't tolerate it despite being in an Indian hair-cutting saloon where freedom of expression is doubly guaranteed. More than what the Constitution does.

Rahul now queried Nitin on the latter's family's stay in their locality. "No, we will have to move to Gurgaon. Yaar my Dad is retiring naa." Nitin said with a sense of remorse. Rahul again chipped in," You may not then enjoy the perks available to you, as they are available to your dad now?" "Certainly not. But I'll get rid of this stupid car-driver who has been shadowing me like a spy, since I will then stay in Delhi as a PG (paying guest)! said Nitin.

At this juncture a lean and weather beaten man entered and asked Nitin, "Aren't you done as yet son?" Nitin looked at the man and blurted: "No Dad. But couldn't you have waited and had patience with yourself? I am 23 now." The man swallowed the reprimand and sunk in the bench. Rahul turned his face towards the man and said, "Oh sorry uncle! We had been talking about you only." There was no comment from Nitin's side.

And what had they been talking about Nitin's father? I thought I should tell the man. But something held me back. A fatherly feeling? Or being reminded how the youngsters threw out of the running train a boy called Manish just a few days back? I don't know. Harried, I hurried homeward.

## The Meridian Divide

India has too many crorepatis these days compared to the past when even a lakhpati was recognised as the son of a “twice-born”. My experience last New Year’s eve compels me to think whether real happiness lives this side or that of the meridian, that answers to the calling of “class” in the capitalist world.

We got passes for the 31st December celebrations at a five-star hotel in the Capital. We were excited to be a part of the much-hyped extravaganza. Our little family made a small group, and made it to the gaiety-gymnasium past 10 pm. The flash-lights beamed in succession from different angles and played their gremlin-game in a multi-coloured range of spectrum, lighting up the revelers’ faces in diverse hues every now and then. The tapping of the dancers’ feet made music with the DJ’s dexterous fingers while near-licentious looks felicitated one another. It was gratification of sorts, with not even a modicum of “concealment”.

The meridian-moment arrived and the entire gathering went into a frenzy, bidding good-bye to the old year that was a new year only 364 days back. Welcome 2003! Happy New Year! Handshakes, bear hugs, embraces, instant and excited calls were being made and received on cellphones. Everything was there. But I noticed that one-to-one greetings were restricted to members of only the self-same group, big or small. None seemed to be genuinely interested in greeting a reveler who was a stranger. Persons beyond acquaintance were deliberately chosen, not to be felicitated; or so it appeared to me.

We decided to rush homeward. Stewards, bearers and staff on the way back accosted us. Our small pack was ushered out and the guards, bellboys and the tall, show-cased sentinels, wearing huge turbans, all invoked the lady luck for us in 2003. We started walking towards the parking-lot outside the hotel. The drizzle, which couldn't dampen the spirit of the merry-makers throughout the day, had stopped. But a chill wind almost pierced through.

Some youngsters, who couldn't secure an entry apparently for the lack of money, were dancing in rustic exuberance, as if to avenge for their hard-luck in the year gone by. They too hailed us. The parking-lot attendant had a muffler round his face and I could see droplets of condensation of the freezing wind, settled on his broomy moustache, when he signalled and helped us pull the car out. He too wished us a happy new year. Reaching home, the domestic help wished each one of us in his Nepali accent: "Naya shaal mubarik hou."

Till I retired for the day with a wish-list of hopes and dreams, something in my mind was troubling me. Why can't the rich tide over their islander-mentality and cut across the tiny worlds of their own creation, of self-proclaimed superiority?"

And why are the comparatively poorer people always so willing to please others, with their humane gentleness, character and disposition? Real happiness does not live on this or that side of the meridian; it is all-encompassing and all-pervasive.

## Two Nights and Three Days

I had hardly made myself comfortable on the office seat when a sweet voice called me up on the phone in a completely western accent. "Could I talk tooooo (reading from her notes) Mr. Deswal, please?" "Yes, speaking," "Oh, good morning sir. I am to inform you, and congratulations for that, you have won a two-nights and three-days free package to any one of the five star hotel destinations in North India, including the one in Kathmandu, Nepal!" "How Come!" I reacted in natural excitement trying to match the artificial, seemingly zealous tone of the caller.

"Your telephone number has been picked up randomly by our computer for a publicity campaign launched by our company. And all you have to do is to come and collect your package and some gifts, spend your evening with us in a hotel. In a short while, my boss will confirm to you the offer. Also, sir, you will have refreshments at the hotel." I literally pinched myself to know if I had really risen from my morning slumber and wasn't enjoying the pleasant offer in a dream.

Next thing I was to immediately do was inform the wife back at home. She too jumped at the information as if we had hit a jackpot or so we thought. I could feel her exuberance and a lifting out of herself on the phone itself when she even suggested quickly: "Isn't it verily too long since we visited Nainital darling! Or shall we go to Nepal... But no...Nainital should be all right!" She herself withdrew as if recovering reflexively, probably recalling what had happened in the Himalayan kingdom not very long back.

I had hardly put down the receiver when the phone bell rang again with the boss in the Chain of Hotels Company himself being on the line. He gave us a code-Shimla 919—after the fashion of the underworld people who share a coded message before delivering some article etc. to confirm the identity of the receiver.

We were supposed to tell the receptionist the code on reaching the hotel so that we did not have any problem in reaching the exact venue without the hassles while entering a five star status building which normally fills you up with some sort of an inferiority complex and you start fumbling with words in English even while talking to the waiters and stewards.

Hoping to do full justice to the refreshments, which we thought we could substitute with our near dinner largesse, we made it on time to the hotel. The hotel staff on being informed by us that we had been invited by such and such company did not extend the usual courtesy expected while receiving a genuine customer. We were signaled to the basement through a dingy stair. On the counter were sitting three representatives of the company who made us fill about half a dozen forms giving minute details about ourselves. I sort of murmured my code in the ears of one of the men on the counter, which met with a cold response as if it was not at all required. I began being suspicious.

We were then ushered into a room where about a dozen tables were laid and on each of them were sitting couples in conversation with the company representative. A smart boy joined us. Shook hands and began grilling us *a la* the C.B.I. investigators as if we had masterminded a serious scam of the denomination and dimensions the politicians and the high and mighty are often accused and capable of.

One full hour passed in out questioning on our income, interest in holidaying etc. and there was no sign of the refreshments being served. Hesitatingly, I asked for a cup of tea and got it after our interviewer painstakingly arranged it. All we were informed about was if we could "buy" the company's "free holiday package". Repeatedly I asked him if we could know the price we had to pay for the satisfaction of the footloose traveler in each of us. The boss was called in who announced it was "just a couple of lakhs for whole 20 years to come and that too at about hundreds of destinations all the world over not to talk of India."

Almost frozen in our seats, my wife and I had no courage left in us to even look into each other's eyes hearing about the cost. We wanted to wind up when the representatives too had made up their minds that we could be excused since we, in their correct estimation, were not the stuff "customers" are made up of.

While taking leave we wanted to collect our promised small package. It said that during the two nights and three days stay at the hotel of our choice at the desired destination we shall have to have two meals which was "compulsory" and each meal would make us shell out a thousand bucks. "Then this is not a free tour package. Our stay like this would compensate the hotel for the lodging charges", I protested and accused the company of having spoiled our evening.

"But in lieu of the evening spent with us, we are giving you two nights package, sir!" The representative said. Disgusted I retorted: "And what is free with these two nights my dear?" "Three days, Sir." Quipped the man on the counter.

Needless to say we did not talk to each other on the way back and had to forgo the dinner since we had already given the cook a free evening in the hope we would really get a free holiday package.

## Of the Mind's Eye

The Face on the wall, and the Shivling at Baba Amarnath Cave could be well termed as the play of the supernatural—of the bizarre and the uncanny—but what about those amazing patterns we find in rocks, clouds, and pealed or shed plaster?

As a child I would often lie on the grass, face upwards, studying the many shapes clouds would take. There would be bears, chariots, flowers, dragons, puppies—even angels. And even as I looked, the cottony bear in the deep blue would change into a horse. Those were moments to savour. Maybe now I do not study clouds as often as I used to then. Given the many chores that have to be packed in the limited time available, there is little time left for as ideal a dalliance as cloud watching. But then whenever I get an opportunity, I grab the chance to study the way Nature plays with its creation.

At times we come across discernible shapes taken by chips that dot the floor, the paint on the wall the little damp spot near the tap in the bathroom, by the trees (especially if stuck by lightening or infested with termites), and, of course, rocks. Why, even the play of light and shade has much to offer. Trees, withered stems, clouds, logs, shrubs artists find great satisfaction in lugging back huge pieces of driftwood to polish and mount with fanciful little bras plaques reading "Dying Tiger", "Mermaid" or for that matter "Birth"—anything they see in the twisted shape. Well, such pieces can be just about anything. What matters is perception—the angle from which one looks at them. To a discerning eye, the contours, depressions and elevations on a surface, silhouettes with a definite and distinct backdrop, all formulate certain forms or at least create a semblance of them.

A rational mind will dub it as the handiwork of what we call denudation, wind effect, a handiwork of water as it brushes stubbornly against the rocks, and because of the sudden change in temperature. Whatever be the reason, it is here that the visual and the visualized concur to give an impression of the forms to an interested onlooker.

We humans are vain creatures. Anything that remotely resembles us, we find fascinating. Well, Nature perhaps is aware of that fact. No wonder we come across patterns that bear an uncanny resemblance to a human body.

If you have been to Mount Abu, a salubrious hill resort in Rajasthan, then you should be familiar with those distinct rocks—Toad Rock, Nun Rock, Camel's Back and Lovers' Rock. Tourists throng these spots to experience the thrill of the fusion of the mortal and the abstract.

The Toad Rock appears as though ready to leap into the 135 feet deep waters of the Nakkhi Lake from a height of 1,000 feet. Many honeymooning couples can be seen near the Lovers' Rock. These two rocky forms appear as though embracing each other—forever in love. And there is the Nun (Rock) eternally preaching eternity.

If you have ever climbed up to Parshuram's temple perched high on its forested hillside and looked down on Renuka Lake, which is supposed to be a huge watery female figure...well, you'll understand that such perceptions are very much a "seeing and believing" experience.

Or if you have a look at the once-in-a-while-appearing distant snowcapped peaks while on your way to Badrinath, you will definitely recall those vast silhouettes known as hathi, ghora and palki. Or how about the trishul? Seen from Cheena Peak just outside Nainital, one sees a distant mountain that does indeed appear to be Shiva's three-pronged weapon.

Likening the beloved to the moon or child to the stars is common...just clichés, really. But those who see castles in the clouds, gnarled hands in the tangled roots of a pine, grazing buffaloes in a heap of boulders, these are the people truly blessed with imagination—like that sculptor played by Jitendra in Geet Gaya Patharon Nain: *Pathar pe kar shayree, Tujhko hamara salaam.*

## The Two-Fingered Comment

A mouse-hunt with the servant takes on unexpected political dimensions as I discover the real meaning of "V"

The 9 O'clock news had just finished... nominations had been filed that day and the clips showed one politician after another coming out of Election Office chambers. Each one of them grinned from ear to ear, raised his arms prizefighter style and flashed the Churchillian "V".

A flip of the channel and there was that wacky "ishtihar" in which thousands of Indian postmen chanted "wee!, wee!" as their leader spelled out his demands. (Or could they have been French postmen chanting "oui, oui" ??) They waved a slightly different selection of pinkies, but the idea is the same.

That was when we heard that faint rustling by the window that signaled the entry of the mouse. Through the small hole meant for filling water, across the grass matting and through the plastic grid at the front: the only way into the room was through the cooler and this tiny mouse had found it. Very clever. Unfortunately for him (her?) I do not like mice, not even clever ones, and this one had been clever once too often.

I rolled up a newspaper, and motioned our servant, Ramu, to grab the broom and station himself by the cooler. The mouse gave me a good 10 minutes of exercise as it dashed from corner to corner. Meanwhile Ramu demonstrated the educational impact of cable television, exclaiming in rapid succession: “Aha!”, “Oye” and “Shit!” depending on how close I had come to hitting the mouse.

Finally I hit on a fiendish plan to “fan” it to death. We gave the critter a chance to get back to the cooler and at the very moment it leapt inside, I turned on the cooler. It worked, the execution signaled by a spatter of blood. Delighted and excited, Ramu’s hand went up in the familiar V-sign.

Now it was his turn to be thrown out of the room.

Over tea-and-newspaper the next morning, I asked Ramu where he picked up that “V” gesture and what he understood by it.

I was in for another surprise. Ramu hunched his shoulders up almost touching his ears and blew the two-note whistle familiar to all watchers of western TV serials.

“Everybody does it,” Ramu explained, Chandraswami, S.K. Jain, Kalpnath Rai, Phoolan Devi...everybody.” And what a list of “every bodies” he had come up with! Nevertheless, I was impressed with how well informed he was.

But he hadn’t finished answering my question yet. When that mouse got in the fan I made a “V” for victory but also because both of us killed that mouse. This sign means hum...'we'. We did it.

I had been wrong to take Ramu for a simpleton. He knew very well what it meant and had even given the gesture a more complex interpretation revolving around joint participation...or possibly complicity, connivance, conspiracy. "We" did it.

Not a bad assessment either. It came back to me how often, as I watched scamsters and thugs flashing the "V" sign, I had thought that their continued reign was a reflection on all of us, that they were symptoms of a much deeper, broader degeneration.

Ramu had shown his political sophistication. Those who beam hour after hour of propaganda at the Ramu's of this country take them for fools. But Ramu knows: "V" is not only for victory, it is "We" and "We" implies, I too. Parteners in sin!

## Bar Counsel

A Golden-eagle was scouting around near a pub in a wet zone and was wonder struck to hear and see the goings-on at an assemblage of empty containers, heaped outside the pub.

Lo and behold! True and faithful spirits in the form of little jinnies came out of their bondage and started a brain-storming session on Bacchus. The sounds from this pile of containers, now empty, indicated as if they were relieved of being instrumental in the falling of a curse of making people go mad with the consumption of the liquid they had been carrying for varying numbers of years to add to the taste of inebriated tongues, in each case.

Godfather chaired the meeting with Aristocrats, Diplomats, and Red-Knights. To represent the clergy, certain Old Monks were present. In his keynote address, Peter Scot threw a Royal Challenge before the assembly that since a tiny but modern state in India had now gone dry, they should find some other greener palm(ed) beeches and leave the state to cater to the glory of its Antiquity of culture and civilisation.

McDowell complained of having been taken for a ride on the rocks as also being used with a lower class stuff called soda. At the mention of "lower class" a Black Patridge joined issue to be encountered by a Rosy-Pelican. They felt uncomfortable, but since they were really the Officer's Choice, present there, a Diplomat, sensing trouble, cooled them with a Royal Salute winking at the Colonel Special with a Red Label put on his lapel to impress.

In the din, the Teachers preached, with the Old Monks in unison, to bedeck and bind the rest of the containers housed in the barred cellars with Blue Ribands to be gifted to the devotees of Bacchus in wet lands, not far away from the dry area.

At the mention of "dry", the dry-gin(ni) looked askance and gesticulated to provoke soda, Soda, already hurt, complained that for no fault of his, he had to bear the graffiti and ugly remarks like "bottoms up", and "one for the road types".

Now Godfather realised that with all the cacophony, the situation was going out of control, and he called Johny Walker to bring along the Bagpiper for the chorus to be sung.

The chorus heralded dawn, and the sweeper, with a long broom, brushed them all in a dumper. Having been so hit, they said with one voice, "All hail prohibition!"

## Pen(ny)-wise

A news-item some time ago compelled me to modify the meaning and update the "expansion" of an abbreviation—VIP, at least for myself.

The information reaching us was about how costly (unthinkable, unbelievable and, of course, unaffordable) pens did make VIPs feel proud of having these in their pockets?

The VIP thus got expanded, in my understanding of the abbreviation, to "Very Important Pen-owners".

Having had a negative stimulation, I took out the costliest pen in my stock of "gifts". And lo, I too found myself to be a very important pen-owner.

The "literature" supplied with "the world's finest writing instrument" of a company as old as a century and a half proclaimed to its user (after formal congrats!), "It is essential that you take a few minutes to read the instructions..." because "your fountain pen is a precision writing instrument and special care is required to ensure a lifetime of writing pleasure."

The Do's, inter alia, suggested, "If you received your fountain pen as a gift, confirm that the nib-size suits your writing style...!" I wondered if the gifted could be choosers too!

The Dont's included, to my liking, "Do not lend your fountain pen to others, for different writing styles and pressures may alter your pen's characteristics". I appreciated the emphasis on "personalisation", for reasons impersonal.

The "literature" went on to enlighten me on how to assemble different accessories and make it a "complete pen" as also that there are nibs (supplied with the pen) of a broader medium size, fine and extra fine. Then there was a chapter on how to clean the pen with a warning that such and such ink would "ruin your pen".

There was yet another chapter on trouble-shooting: "Should a situation arise when your pen is not performing properly, this guide should help you remedy it. If the situation persists, take it to our nearest service centre in New York, London, Paris, Los Angeles, Detroit, Boston, Chicago, Washington D.C.....!"

I don't know when my "gifted" pen will make me the VIP of sorts who could afford to airdash to the places listed above, get it repaired and land back in Hisar (Haryana), of all the places in India!

## Blue Mysteries

One of the recognised astrologers of the country proclaimed that blue would be the colour of the new millennium. After hearing this, my mind was all set to explore the blue world.

Why is a woman keenly interested in literary pursuits called a blue-stocking? Why is the blood flowing in the veins of members of royal families called blue? Why is the hard-so-swat big fly termed bluebottle?

Why is making an appearance or doing things after long intervals said to be doing so, "once in a blue moon"? Why is a product on celluloid with porn details dubbed a blue film? Why is something untoward labelled as "a bolt from the blue"? Why is a blue ribbon always a mark of distinction? Why does a depressed man look blue?

Only an athlete representing his institution can wear a blue scarf or a blue cap. Why? Why is a sea-man called a blue-jacket? Why are hardships and inconvenient things termed blue? Why is a loyal member of a party called "true-blue"?

Why, in business and finance, is a stock that is considered strong and reliable in terms of dividend yield referred to as a blue-chip? And in the computer era, why should a blue-chip control your daily routine?

Why is a murderer of children called a "blue-beard"? Why is "blues" the nomenclature given to melancholy lyrics which are tales of woe or unhappy love in African-American music? Why does a blueprint deserve that appellation in making plans before they are executed?

That should be enough, I think. And blue is not only blue. It's navy-blue, sky-blue, ocean-blue, British-blue, Oxford-blue, Cambridge-blue and so on. If I were to pluck a piece from the sky, it might not be blue, yet it looks blue.

Nearer home, in Hindu mythology, Lord Shiva is believed to have swallowed the poison that emerged after the sagar manthan. When the poison reached the throat of Shiva, he retained it there because if it had been gulped down, the Devtas residing in his stomach would have been endangered.

Hence, *Neelkanth* is appellation given to Lord Shiva's throat, which turned blue as a result of harnessing the deadly poison. And since poison, in all its form, when it affects the human body, turns it to blue, no edible stuff was given this colour by Mother Nature. The fathomless depth of the oceans confirms the profundity of blue.

The vastness of the expanded skies proclaims the infiniteness of blue. The blue-shift in the spectrum exhibits its frequency and intensity in a striking manner. And all that is even described as blue, as we have seen, may not at all be blue. Surely then, here it becomes mystifying.

Blue is not the colour to eat. Hence, no blue rasgullas; no blue cheese! Any takers!

## That Extraa Day

Tomorrow someone may tell you, “It’s my 18$^{th}$ birthday and I am 72 years old.” In the first instance it may sound absurd but on consciously being aware of that “extraa” leap in the almanac, you may well take it on its face.

Care for this rhyme:

“Thirty days hath September,
April, June and November;
All the rest have thirty-one,
Excepting February alone;
Which hath but twenty-eight, in fine,
Till leap year gives it twenty-nine.”

To resolve the past irregularities Julius Caesar with the advice of an astronomer Susigenes figured out that a year of 445 days was needed to do a balancing act between Time and Earth. And that long year was 46 B.C. Thus the leap year began in circa 47 B.C.

In the 8th century an Anglo-Saxon monk by the name Bede found that the Julian year was longer by 11 minutes and 14 seconds but nothing could be done about it till the 15th century when Pope Gregory XIII decreed in favour of astronomer

Christopher Clavius' calculations. Thus 11 days were totally eliminated by making October 4 followed by October 15 in 1582 A.D. since months and seasons were not matching as worked out. Accordingly, December was made the last month of a year with a leap year to follow every four years on February 29. And a new Gregorian Calendar came into force.

For the reason that the spring equinox determines the date of Easter, the Christians had a stage in having a stable calendar, which the entire world still follows. Hindu festivals are determined by Vikrami and Samvat almanacs; the Muslims follow Hijri.

There are about four-million leapies (born on Febuary 29th) in the world. Our own Morarji Bhai was one of these. In Scotland in the year 1288, the Leap Year Balls, held in glamorous and romantic settings, afforded an opportunity for women to legally propose to their men of choice. Prior to this, in $5^{th}$ Century Ireland, there existed this practice of allowing women to propose to men on February 29 and in case the latter refused, they were fined.

Simple minds question the astronomical logic of adding a day to the month of February only. One Jacob E. Goldman wrote to the editor of The New York Times, on January 5 1995, about a linguistic inconsistency saying, that the 'extraa' day should be added at the end of the year i.e., 31st December and it need not be referred to as the leap day; rather a leap year. How silly! What will happen to the New Year Eve and the New Year Day Mr. Jacob? Shall we then say, "A Happy New Leap Year to you!"

Aquarians of the world, unite to continue having a day still added to February for who knows a Caesar or a Gregory may alter the almanac. And the leapies, A Very Happy Birthday to you all in advance!

## A Branch of Bonding

Every time gifts are exchanged, a lot of thinking precedes the actual event. This is true, though, with people who care to consider making a real present.

Be it birthday celebration, a festival, or an anniversary, the exchange of gifts gets a mindful thought. What should be bought?" What should be suitable? Does its value match what had been gifted to you earlier by the same person? And, above all, does it suit the occasion? These are some of the considerations behind a gift that lights up the recipient's face when a good gift changes hands.

Last year on our marriage anniversary we received a unique gift from our immediate neighbours, Mrs. and Mr. Sprat Herbert Mohan. Mohan is the son of the English journalist and Indian freedom fighter, late Mr. Phillip Sprat, who was tried, in the famous Meerut Conspiracy case. Mr. Sprat had married a Hindu Shivite Brahmin girl from the present-day Tamil Nadu. We had invited their son Sprat Herbert Mohan and his family for dinner on that day. Mohan, initially a soldier, joined the police and rose to become a Director General.

All of a sudden, around eight in the evening, we heard a sound as if something was being transported to our house. Thud-thud-thud. And there were the Sprats carrying a heavy, potted, rubber plant.

"Many happy returns of the day," they chorused their greetings to us while still panting and gasping for breath. All our guesses as to what the Sprats would gift us were put to rest as the pot itself.

We could never think up in our wildest imagination that even a potted plant could be a wedding anniversary gift! Or so we thought.

We started taking good care of the 'planted present' and at same time tried to read meanings into the unique present. Whether it stood for prosperity, prolificity and purity! Whether it symbolised an everlasting freshness of relations!

What messages are its dark but attractive leaves to unfold? We will have to keep watering the figurative plant of relations lest it should wither away! One after the other, these thoughts kept tickling our imagination and we discussed them very often.

If this gift had been something else and not the rubber plant, definitely we would have forgotten it soon after the occasion itself, as is the case with many such gifts. We admire the Sprats who gifted this greenery of thoughts to us, which has been not only a pleasant thing to look at but also a warm sensation to feel the presence of the Sprats around us even after they have retired and settled at a distant place.

The other day when I was gently cleaning the leaves of the plant with a soaked cloth. I wondered about the size the gift had grown to. "The pot would prove to be inadequate for the plant in the coming weeks". I thought to myself. And my son, standing by my side, said, as if reading my thoughts, "Shall we transfer this plant to the orchard in our village?" I nodded in the affirmative. How much we have converged on the growing gift through our common care of the plant!

We transferred the plant to our small orchard in the village where it has grown into a big tree now. And equally tall do the Sprats stand in our memory whenever we visit our native place and cast a look at the once gifted and now growing tree.

The Sprats did really rope in their branch of bonding to our family tree. Can't I call it a family tree? I think I can.

## Related Events

I know exactly what I was doing when the Indian Parliament was attacked on December 13. I also know where I was when Colombia crashed and the Twin Towers crumbled. Older people remember attack on Pearl Harbour, and nearer home, when the port of Cochin was bombarded. Many can still recall the grant of Indian Independence.

This may be true of the highbrow types but how did the humble folks generally remember dates and events? Births and deaths and their timing. Fierce floods or fire, as also epidemics. Well, everything that was eventful was related to another event, which affected either everyone, or a particular individual. No time but space existed for them.

My great grandmother used to tell us her marriage was as old as the big jamun tree in our village for it was planted the same month of Sawan. She could never have known her date of birth but yes she did recall who all perished in Kaatakwali—an epidemic that struck the areas in 1930s. Also even before that, when a freebooter plundered the Jind areas and met with severe resistance from the local Jats.

Grandfather had his stories to relate, timing them to the two world wars and the Indian soldiers who fought for the British in foreign lands. He also gave us vivid details of one such soldier who developed an affair with a white Mem while in Italy and that she insisted on coming to India in such fierce manner that she lay prostrate in front of the vehicle carrying him. I do not really know whether he was jealous.

Later generation people remember the traumatic Maar-kaat—the blood bath—of Partition of the country. Who killed how many and how many got butchered? What families were uprooted and what were allotted lands on this side? Who was looted and who rolled in riches after chasing the fleeing families? Frenzied rantings of Allah-o-Akbar and Har-Har-Mahadev still reverberate in the ears of many who can relate the life's events to those days of utter anarchy.

Simpler episodes were linked to occurrences like when there was a big breach in the canal that flooded the areas or crops having failed due to famines. A marriage in some landlord's household or the local heroes' exploits too timed certain events. Levying of taxes or a general deference, made news.

Then there were the events like a dacoity with murder at a rich man's haveli with which the other simpletons would mark happenings concerning themselves, Saangs, modified to swangs these days, which were rostrum-performances, by eminent local artists, also marked their time. Ruralites assembled in huge numbers to watch these. Sometimes such events ended with brawls and free fights giving ample titillation to the episodes to be remembered by all and sundry.

Other softer options of sensing or estimating time with the villagers were the early twitter of the birds, or the crowing of a cock; or if it was dead of night, the howling of the jackals or the owls' yowl. The sun and the moon also guided them with their positions.

I remember a rattle-brain who was given a watch in dowry. Many in the village laughed at his flaunting it on the wrist. Still others asked him time more to tease than to know the time. This made him show them the watch since he did not know how to read time himself. And in vogue still is having a watch tattooed on your wrist.

It seems time remained tattooed in the psyche of the humble folks while space did have some suppositions to vaguely count on. But who the hell was then bothered about either time or space?

## Mango Manners

Sophistication and eating mangoes do not go together. And with so many varieties of the king of fruits, each having its own culinary protocol, it becomes all the more difficult to "execute them tastefully".

The best way to eat mangoes, as they say, is to consume them without wearing anything on your person, for the obvious reasons of sullying and soiling. Neither can you hold it too tight nor too loose; and the seed may slip out of the hand to land anywhere, even on your clothes.

Different varieties have different skin texture with various hues of green yellow and red. The stones also vary, from paper thin to annoyingly big.

The desi fashioned gnawing of fibrous seed had its own advantages. The deeper you bury your teeth the more juice flows into your mouth. This attempt to retrieve a mango after the method of the Epicureans is, in fact, the best way to do justice to the mango and its eating discipline.

There are many popular varieties available like dussehri, langra, saroli, safeda, tota, chausa, sunchri, alfanso, kalmi, et. al. These varieties do not ripen at the same time to afford you an opportunity to taste different varieties at the same time.

The last to arrive in the market is the gadha variety or the "donkey like". It is very fat and tasteless, but it gives you the vicarious pleasure of the times when you ate real mangoes and not the "ass of a mango".

Some eat mangoes after cutting them into pieces using forks. Others would have them sliced in a way that the skin on one side is intact. Still others like me want to have the entire skin peeled off and eat it like a laddoo.

An interesting thing happened with us on board an Aeroflot flight. We were served dussehri mangos considering that most of the passengers were Indians. A Westerner who had not obliged me with exchanging his window seat was at his wits' end on how to peel and eat it. He had probably never tasted the fruit before.

I exchanged glances with my better half and nudged her indicating she "should not eat her fruit yet, lest the boy should get a cue." I confess, I became a bit too cruel to the boy out of mischief. We watched him eat his mango.

He put it on a plate. Took the knife in his right hand and with a little pressure held it and then pierced the mango skin with the fork. This made a juicy sprout shoot which landed on his cheeks. Cleaning himself with a tissue and licking the soiled fork and knife, he gave another unsuccessful try. Then he gave up.

Then it was our turn. We took the mangoes in our hands like a soft toy. Removed the acidic and bulbous top and started sucking the juice with a slurping noise in our typical desi style. The boy kept looking of the window with his mind focused on our mangoes and the way they were eaten.

Before landing, we thought we had scored a point over a representative of the race, which introduced their cutlery to us.

## Story of Idiot Box

Notwithstanding my association with many a 'reported' dowry death since my birth in India, I proudly claim the status of the birth-giver to the so-called culture erosion syndrome in this heritage-(un) conscious country.

Yes, I am "Teevee", alias the idiot box, alias the small screen!

Take care to have a look at the time of my "import"? I remember scores of adults, no to talk of children, clinging to the windows and singing serenades like lovers of yore, while the room I was placed in was jam-packed with my "watchers". In those days people used to count on their fingers the freshly installed antennae at housetops to add to their general knowledge of the number of my likes brought in various households. And an antenna on a house added to the social and financial status of the owner in those days.

As a prized possession, I was housed in the drawing-rooms at that time, and although I was a cure for the mothers-in-law and a curse for the brides, I kept my admirers glued to me even if I was showing them a Kuchipudi performance or a shehnai vadan by Ustad Bismillah Khan. I can still recall the traumatic interruption of those days, and the bright side of such a situation was that the viewers had no option to 'channel' their disgust on any other route. Whatever I had, was sold out, and was considered valuable.

With the hosting of ASIAD in Delhi, my apartheid complexion was made colourful. Thereafter, I did not have to look back since they loaded me with serials, song programmes, sports items and late night movies.

With the introduction of the last mentioned stuff of nocturnal delight, I found my way into my master's bedroom. I can confide that it was at this juncture that I got linked up with my bosom friend "We-See-Are", sometimes sending my "blue blood" go pita-pat.

Good heavens! Here the peeping holes provided me with an escape route, and the teenagers came to my rescue. Now I have become a favourite of the new generation alike and the toddlers.

They drew me out of their parents' bedrooms and honoured me with the living-rooms and lobbies. Again, I was the one who united the family and strengthened the bonds of love. I overcame the generation gap and filled it with "twinkling stars, zealous beams, see none showers".

I have come a long way and graduated myself to be need perception of my lovers. They now prefer to have two of us in a family; of course, if they can afford a decent living without company.

At times I feel shivers running down my "spy-in" if I am reminded of the Anti-TV Club that was formed in Bonn in Germany in the seventies.

I fail to understand why my critics always curse me for having enabled the Indians to sever their connection with their so-called roots, culture, heritage, etc.! I too have lost my links with the Indian stations in preference to the satellites. "*Zamaney kay saath chalo*!"

## Before & After *Maha-Vinash*

Ignorance may be bliss and the ignorant may be blissfully unconcerned with the goings-on around them, but the way the "informed" people are cheated baffles me.

Yes, definitely they are cheated because nothing really happened despite all the inputs in the media and the entire extravaganza related to this aspect of awe-inspiring and frightening news, even when the possibility of comet Tempel-Tuttel's entering the satellites' path was something between 0.01 and 0.03 per cent.

Of course, it is a great relief that nothing really happened but a little insight into the human psyche will prove my point of apprehension that the homo-sapiens are sensitive to and respond to the stimulus in many ways—including excretions like perspiration and secretion of adrenalin—coupled with the palpitation of sorts.

Surely, there are innumerable suns and stars in the entire universe and their crossing of paths with each other should make news. But apprehensive and white-livered people postpone their transactions, put off marriages to later dates, push ahead ceremonies and wait for the catastrophe.

Well, holocaust, fireworks, total destruction, etc., are weak and thus inappropriate expressions when it comes to the vernacular projection of "Maha-vinash" at least for the common Indian. Whenever there is news of celestial disturbance—constellation crosses, planets' path-breaking, etc.—it is natural for informed human beings to be apprehensive.

Remember the well-known "sky-lab" which earned a niche for itself in the temple of 'terr(a) or'-firma! Anything really falling from above to destroy something has verily come to deserve the appellation the "sky-lab" since then.

And remember the total solar eclipse of the eighties, when pictures of crows almost squatting and merry-making on the otherwise busy roads of the erstwhile Connaught Place in the Capital were published by newspapers the following day because information was made available that an unusual discharge of radiation could blind one instantaneously.

Doordarshan, I remember, had sought successfully to keep the TV viewers indoors for the whole day when Rishi-Dimple starrer "Bobby" and Dharmendra-Sharmila paired "Chupke-Chupke" were telecast that day. But this was to take care of the informed, and not the ignorant. The latter enjoyed the bliss of a sudden and strange happening and did not feel cheated even in the face of experiencing night-like darkness during the daytime. They rather had the thrill of bewilderment and reward.

I also remember, as a child in the sixties, when "ashtha-grihas" (eight planets) were to "rub shoulders" with one another and create fireworks that could lighten up (?) the whole sky and produce booms like thunders. The experience of my teens is still fresh in memory, and precisely for this reason my heart is gripped by fear, like every other informed person, every time there is some news of celestial disturbance.

And it is then that I am reminded of Wordsworth, who exclaimed: there was a time "when meadow, grove and earth did seem to me appareled in celestial light..."

Well, the celestial light shall lighten up (including the pun) only the blissfully ignorant mind and not those bombarded with information. The latter is only a cheated person. Why should we seek information and feel cheated even in matters "heavenly"?

## Born on the Roadside

There is a peaceful assembly of people on the roadside and an issue is being discussed. "Hey! What is the matter?" cries someone. And lo! The leader is born. The matter would be explained to him and he would listen with utmost attention, quite concerned and involved. If any initiative is required, he would offer his services, whether it is arguing with somebody, (and in a worse situation), or fighting, as the occasion demands.

The leader has the capacity to carry the crowd with him and is endowed with the ability to convince the gathering, putting forth his own viewpoint. Since there is no better alternative, his assertion is honoured. Even if there is any other suggestion, he would see to it that it is relegated and discarded.

This type of leader has a very short life-span, limited only to that particular issue's intricacies. It is still possible that in a similar situation another leader is born in place of the previous one, and the logic put forth by the latter may again be well received by the gathering, even if it is in total defiance of the one advanced earlier.

The leader born on the roadside is not a hypocrite always. Rather he does have in him qualities like comradeship, pleasing ability, selflessness and even charity (at a condition of no dividends). His job at times has a no-profit-no-loss basis.

If you have a genuine, common problem with the conductor in a bus and the latter is an unrelenting type, it is possible that your friend, the leader, is sitting just by your side. Maybe, he is not an aggrieved party, yet he would poke in his nose to relieve yours. He would be ready to see any available officer, to espouse your cause as also to assure you that he would stand by you as a witness, if the matter assumes proportions warranting approaching of the court.

Sometimes the services offered by this leader prove to be beneficial to all. For example, if there is no queue before a ticket window, he would jump from nowhere and make the people line up, using his self-acquired authority. This leader always has a winning attitude towards the suddenly cropped-up problem by having the gathering on his side and ultimately prevailing upon the trouble-maker.

People in difficult situations look forward to the emergence of a roadside leader and have a relieving sigh.

## And Now Fifth Estate

They say with guarantee that there would be no fourth world war. Why? Because the world would be destroyed in the third war.

By the same argument, there would be no Sixth Estate. Why? Because the world would be fully exposed by the Fifth Estate.

But where does that Fifth Estate exist? Well, it is already born and has started making its impact. The only thing, which remains is its recognition.

Four video-tapes created waves in Uncle Sam's land with all those lewd details and near-porno stuff (deposition?), and the curiosity with which TV viewers all the world over watched the telecast is sufficient evidence to prove supra-channel superiority, the existence of the Fifth Estate.

A cartoon appeared in a newspaper depicting no sale of tickets in American movie halls since the tapes were scheduled to go on air that day.

Wise men say you don't feel any binding (yes, literally) on you while you are in the bathroom, and all naked to yourself only. The moment you come out, you need covers. Your family members or society at large might object.

But how if by some "system" you are exposed. You may not need the bathrooms then. Thus the might of the "system" or the Fifth Estate is proved, and the question of a Sixth Estate does not arise at all.

Nearer home, a film-critic friend of mine, who bade good bye to the City Beautiful to be in the Bollywood-Bountiful, informed me on the phone the other day about the might of the Fifth Estate.

"The stars don't give the dates for interviews, etc. to newspaper and magazine reporters anymore with all that zeal and enamouring since there are better channels available nowadays", he lamented.

"There was a time when the directors themselves, not to talk of the stars' secretaries, would inform us about 'Madam's desire' to fix up an interview", he said "they would tempt us saying, 'Sir, she would be wearing a revealing dress, rest assured, and certainly with no nakhras and blandishments'..."

But with Star TV, Zee TV, MTV, Channel V, Sony etc. proving to be prowler and popular networks, the celebrities all over the world have come to rate the printed word of the Fourth Estate as having degenerated to being a thing of the past.

Well, the Fourth Estate was surely born at a time when there was no other better medium of reporting.

The media in general may include the "printed word practitioners", but electronic media certainly is the in-thing and is proving detrimental to the interest of the real Fourth Estate.

My film-critic friend recalls those golden days when it was all hunky-dori with the reporters, but these days even the Bollywood stars' secretaries are not available on the phone. If by chance someone is on the line, he would say, "I am sorry, Mr....(earlier it was Sir or Madam). In fact, Madam's mood is very upset these days...You can understand...."

"The same evening", says my friend, "Madam appears on a popular channel brimming, teasing, winking etc."

Even politicians are reported to be visiting five-star hotel saloons for having a haircut when they would be facing the camera, on schedule.

Pen-pushes and readers of the printed word unite, for word-power is giving way to beam-power. And the Fifth Estate is all set to "roll camera".

## Terrorizing Trifles

I have always wondered why some humans are so white livered and timid in mind that in attempting to avoid innocuous and trifling events they break their bones in apprehension of what may be very dangerous, while it is not.

Take for example an ashhill on a cigarette. The smoker might well spill soup on the bystander than let the ash break and drop on the ground. Another instance can be linked to the bathroom where while bathing and rubbing soap on your body, the cake slips out of the hands, you do a near gymnastic feat in an attempt to recover it, as if, it was lost then you would have lost the entire fortune at your disposal.

You know pretty well that, most of the times when you are "presumably" caught between the sliding doors of a lift, than they open automatically, since there is an inbuilt safety mechanism to that effect. But invariably you get upset, and an invading through is noticed, every time you are so "trapped".

And why do people, while traveling in a motor, lean on the other side of the negotiated curve, almost reflexively in a centrifugal way, attempting to be a little safer, knowing full of well that their mass is not sufficient enough to do that balancing act, compared with that of the vehicle in order to audaciously avoid the toppling angle as against the might of mother earth's gravity.

I think the problem has a deep-rooted psychological elucidation. Remember when you were a child and your father, while shaving his chin, had planted a foam swatch, landing from his shaving brush on to your fluffy cheeks? Sure, you had shrieked and cried for mamma to lap you up and say she would beat papa for his browbeat-brushed and nasty mischief played on a lovely little thing. And for the rest of your life it seems, you developed a kind of fear of the terrorizing trifles.

Also, remember how you reacted to the clip-clap of the barber's scissors when your father took you out to his saloon for a hairdo? All the time you were apprehensive of your ear being chopped off and had kept sinking in that made-to-order pedestal on the chair for seating babies.

Certain ex-criminal tribes cash in on this very pusillanimity in the human beings when they devise ways and means to dupe the people at large. Their family members also contribute their bit in the manipulation. Their modus operandi is to employ their children also in the cheating-feat. They would throw the biscuit paste or some other similar substance on the clothes of the subjects, who on finding a dirty thing hurled on them, forget everything around, and would instantaneously, in a hush-hush manner desire an immediate cleansing and riddance. And in so disturbing the subject, the cheats rob them of their belongings, stealthily and with craft.

Well, I am envious of the painter who goes on with his creation on the canvas smearing not only his clothes but hands, face and even hair, quite unmindful of the stokes, which otherwise strike terror in the minds of others—a shade less ordinary. But don't certain painters even wear an apron while "dealing" with colours. Is it really not for seeking a little more liberty with oneself or it is a cover for apprehensions?

Being on the defensive is perhaps a trait with noble hearted human beings, the terrorizing agent being gigantic or trifling, notwithstanding.

## *Mere Wala* Brown

Talking about the "seven sins", Shakespeare mentions a "green-eyed monster" to connote jealousy among human beings. "Gora rung" or fair complexion of the beloved may have been a subjective preference with a few poets while describing the beloved's charms, but there are others also who sing, "*Kahin ek masoom nazuk see larki; Bahut khoobsurat, magar sanwli see*".

"Sanwla" may not be dark but it is definitely "not so fair" and this attribute in the Hindu way of life may be ascribed to "*Sanwra salona Krishan Kanhayya*".

But what about expressions like being "red with rage" or "lal peelay hone"; having a wicked heart or "kale-dil-wala"; turning pale or "peela par jana"; being white-livered or "sookhe jigar wala"; telling a white lie or "safed jhoot bolna"; and so on?

Human beings seem to appreciate with colours not only their skinny appearance but also they will paint certain emotions with different hues. This again is a subject deep-rooted in human psyche.

The best example of this colour bias in human beings is the question of apartheid as also that we call the royal people, possessing veins through which not red but blue blood flows. And why only this that intelligent people have "grey matter" in their brains while everybody else's substance in that protected cavity of the skull is again of the same colour.

Our poets definitely dwell on rosy lips, pink cheeks, a brown cascade of hair, silvery voice, unfathomable ocean-blue eyes, and what not!

While in England in 1992 I came across a very interesting explanation, given by certain Asians, of being the best complexioned race in the Almighty's scheme of things and to His liking.

Having created the homo-sapiens, God decided to give them appropriate colour. He ordered for an oven in which the humans thus created were put to be baked and soaked in a definite pigment.

This oven was opened only to find that the humans were over-baked and they acquired a very dark complexion. "What to do with these...?" God pondered for a while and ordained, "Let them be thrown into Africa and such like places."

Another round of baking was ordered and this time the stuff came out half-baked. God again brooded and said, "Let them be thrown into Europe, America and such like places."

In the third round, perfectly baked brown humans emerged from the oven and a contented Almighty exclaimed with joy, "Oh! Mere wala brown! Let them all be deservedly thrown into that part of the world comprising India, Pakistan, Afghanistan, etc.

Take pride, O' countrymen, in your being the browny race of the Almighty's choice and stop imitating the Westerners and becoming brown-sahibs.

## Misplaced Perceptions

Obviously obsessed with the pretention of studying and knowing literature, a student tells me about the marigold being a "vulgar flower". Taken aback as I am, it is not that easy for me to gulp the bitter potion down the throat, for I am flower-lover.

I ask her to dent an explanation in me for I am not at all willing to accept anything in dishonour of a lovely, full-bloomed, smiling marigold, with each petal proclaiming the tenderness of touch and yellowness of mood.

To make matters worse, this student goes to the extent of calling the marigold "stupid and lecherous". Piqued at this second salvo, I caution her, "Stay on, stay on, young lady. After all, how can the poor thing be lecherous, admitting that in your estimation it may be stupid for one meaning of this adjectival attribute is fool-ish as well. And this phoolish does not make a marigold more flower-like.

These days, I can understand the poets' constraints, in this fast changing world, of not being able to afford and fantasise for daffodils, while 'lying on the couch in a pensive' mood because people nowadays do not venture out to have an aesthetic feast for the soul but for the eyes, in "arranged chrysanthemums (show)". The "exhibitionism" in the flowers does have the better of the onlookers, the so-called flower-lovers. Now I understand how the flowers could be blamed for a "vulgar" show but...?

Do I not now contradict myself like Walt Whitman? And am I not being driven nearer an agreement with the young dame sans mercy for the poor marigold! She, and I too,- both may be right for even Whitman admits, "I am large; I contain multitudes".

Perceptions play pranks and prejudice popular beliefs. Hence everything looks pale to a jaundiced eye. Two and two make four rotis (bread) for a hungry person, and a Dr. Faustus perceives the face of sweet Helen, capable of launching a thousand ships and burning the topless towers of Illume!

For one, Taj Mahal may be an object created to poke fun at the steadiness and consistency of lovers of humble origin. But for another person, it may be the ever-burning candle in the mausoleum of love. (Remember the film numbers (?) "*Ik shehanshah ne banwa ke hasin Taj Mahal, hum garibon ki mohabbat ka udaya hai mazaq*", and "*Taj wo shama hai ulfat ke sanam-khane ki*".

For a Jehangir, Kashmir may be heaven on earth, and for the present day inhabitants, it may be a place to drive oneself away from. Likewise, a marigold may be a stupid or vulgar or even lecherous flower for the young lady, but for me...!

Let me give it another serious thought. I am introspecting, and what I see before my "inner eye" is a pair of shows of a woman removed by the bedside. One shoe is off its so(i)le and is lying parallel to the ground and the other is slightly tilted on the former's side. The scene may be quite suggestive for some, including me.

Well, if I can see lust in a pair of shoes, why can't the young lady perceive the flower, a marigold, to be stupid, vulgar, lecherous and so on. I am still a student of, and she has mastered Literature.

## Wintry Comforts

On a holiday if winter fog envelops everything around you, and you sit smugly in your cozy room wrapped in a shawl or a blanket, you may like to view "Bay Watch" with those macho men and girls diving into the cold water. Then the theory of "imitation" propounded by Aristotle may start making an impact not only on your intellectual plain but even on your physical self. What you can experience, even in that warm wrapping around you, is shivers with clattering teeth.

In India, we need to declare seasons such as wearing woolens or packing them off, respectively, heralds winter and summer, and someone may point out, "Oh...so you have declared...!"

Winters, we not only declare individually or family-wise but also prepare ourselves to combat its severity in many ways. For example, the woolens are dry-cleaned or washed well in advance; certain nuskhas, which are time-tested and unwritten preparations as a panacea for all ills involving eating pure ghee in one form or the other (for it is believed still that it gives you more energy), find their application on cooking utensils; quilts are re-cast and all those room-heaters, etc. are unpacked to face winter's wrath.

I am toying with selling an idea whether the law-makers could understand the need to impose a “razai tax”on the idlers in society. These drones should be issued razais for a limited number of hours, and a complete rationing could be a solution to the problem of “excessive razai using”, thereby creating more mandays during the winters.

In Haryana, there is a saying that jada (cold weather) does not spare even a thanedar. This expression, perhaps, has its roots in the dress code for the cops laid down by the British. Police officers in those days used to wrap woollen putties and anklets from heels to calf-muscles and further upto the knees. Then the entire wrappings were put in khaki socks. Even then if cold weather was severe enough to influence a cop, it confirms that our policemen did have their “Achilles heel” at a time when Human Rights did not chase them, but jada did.

A soldier from Haryana posted at a snowy border picket wrote a letter to his father that since it was too cold there, he needed a razai, also called shayod in the local dialect. The poor father was confused. After giving thought to his son’s “needs”, he concluded that the razai, if it could not be shayod, then surely it was his wife. But this father wrote back to his son that since his razai (and as per the father’s understanding, the soldier’s wife) was away to her parents, he was unable to oblige him. Instead, as a fatherly gesture, he sent five kilograms of ghee for his son, to be able to combat cold weather.

But winter has its advantage too. You may not take bath for any number of days altogether. Your cheeks may not require any "foundation" (cream) and may turn pink naturally. If you have less flesh on your bones, your padded clothes may make you look more presentable.

Well, if winter comes, can comforts be far behind!

## When would the School Start

A teenager mopeding ahead of me suddenly made a U-turn and had a miraculous escape. In that split second, even out of a reflex, I could not think of applying the brakes to save the dare-devil.

My wife sitting by my side turned pale with terror and held her head in her hands. Her reflexes are perhaps better than mine but when she recovered from the shock she could only stutter "Slow, s.l.o.w....s.l.o.w..., the children have their vacations". Otherwise, she can shout loud enough to break your tympanum.

Including a couple of our own there are about 20 children in our immediate neighbourhood. They have formed a group and if it is hot outside, they will all be indoors playing *antakshri.* They will all squat, or lie flat, or roll-over, or dance, on the carpet, and leave it dirty enough to exchange steel utensils for.

Anytime the call-bell may ring and there will not be less than half-a-dozen of them enquiring if our children can also join them. I cannot refuse, after all, they are not asking for the proverbial moon, that too during their "happy days are here again" period.

Over-hearing their conversation, is reassuring: The standard topics are the TV serials, comics, cartoon films, Amitabh, Mithun, Govinda, baggies and loosers, hobby classes and above all *tutak tutak tutian.* In my days it was homework, stamp collection, bell-bottoms, Rajesh Khanna, Jeetendra; *Hare Rama Hare Krishna,* and *Mera babu chhail chhabila.* Things haven't changed much.

Come evening and they form groups, walk hand-in-hand with walkmans, take two or three friends on the pillions and zoom past making zigzags.

Boredom sets in with great rapidity. Best friends are out of station with LTC availing parents. The comic-walla's stock is exhausted several weeks before school begins again. There's "nothing to do"...except vacation homework. But that's what never seems to get done.

And then hardly a day before school reopens... it's time to run to Mom for assistance in completing a mountain of assignments on an emergency basis. Where did all those boring days fly to?

## Easier Said than Done

Have you ever tried to catch a currency note thrown from the first floor of your house? You do a lot of bending here and bending there, stepping a little too far to give you pain in the waist for nearly a couple of months. Still, like the falling pale and dead leaf in autumn, the note may elude you.

Catching butterflies is equally exacting a task, and only children can perform it with skill since they can exert a little more than grown-up people. Similarly, the fly-swatter may hit the target right and reduce it to pulp, but try it with your hand or even with a folded newspaper and see that the task becomes arduous. In the same manner, it seems as if rowing a boat is very easy but it does require sinewy efforts actually.

Looking into the mirror, if you shape up your moustaches you may not be able to always pick the right hair. Many times the hands will automatically make the scissors pluck nastily to give you the looks of person with imperial moustaches. Applying *kajal* in the eyes or, as they do it nowadays, the eye-liner, while looking into the glass again demands dexterity like putting the thread in the needle-hole in one go may be nearly impossible. And you may never learn to tie the knot of a necktie.

While in the bathroom if the soap slips out of your wet hands, it may give you a slip-disc provided you have the tendency similar to the urge of catching a falling star. And also if you have applied soap on your face and the eyes are closed, and if the soap cake slips, it becomes hell of a problem to really lay your hands on it once again.

Well, sneezes and coughs are good hookers when it comes to handling delicate tasks. But when your wife is painting her nails with polish or even applying bindi right in the middle of the forehead, just about whatever suitable distance from the nose-root between the eyebrows, and you happen to either sneeze or even ask her where the keys for the cupboard were at that moment, you are in for trouble because you will be accused of disturbing exactly when the "strike was to be launched".

Even master-stroke players complain of being distracted with sneezes, coughs and yawns when within that fraction of a second the die was about to be cast or the trigger was just to be pressed. A Tamil saying has it that a virgin may go without taking anybody along, but a yawn surely will. People are seen yawning infection to deter the best initiators.

Drivers are not to be spoken to when they are negotiating a curve, particularly in the hills. An electrician is not to be disturbed while holding those red and blue live wires. The barber with his razor on the neck is the most dangerous person to be invited to react to a dialogue. The singer loses his note (sargam and sur) while the tailor, busy with his scissors and making the cloth ready for draping, may cut a little more length than desired if disturbed. Perhaps they all need undisturbed concentration, typical of a busy-bee, while performing an easy looking but difficult task.

Certain tasks seem very easy to perform, but it is actually otherwise. Mark Twain believed that a man who cannot handle his tools is no man. By the same token, if you are not able to replace a fused bulb, you may well question your "handling", if not manhood. Truly, things are easier said than done.

## Grandpa's Remedies

Like most old people, my grandfather too was obsessed with his eating habits. The scientific explanations regarding the futility of traditional foodstuff prescribed for some maladies did not appeal to him.

If he was convinced that lassi was good for the liver, he would drink at least two glasses with breakfast. But he would caution everyone against drinking lassi at dinner time.

He was also very fond of milk and would always sit and drink a big tumbler of milk thrice a day. His explanation for sitting down was, "If you stand and drink milk, it will reach your feet and not benefit the stomach."

Grandpa was a die-hard ghee and butter fan, especially for the young. His recommendation: "If you eat enough ghee in your young age, it will sustain you all through your old age."

For him, cholesterol etc. were useless medical terms. He stressed on the lubricating characteristics ghee, butter and oil provided to the joints and the grease that kept him going. It was his prescription for anyone with cracking joints.

Grandfather loved his drink. And he loved to drink it neat. He recommended eating sweets with liquor. This was perhaps to get an extra kick and was done without knowing that sugar added to alcohol enhanced the effect.

Not only for himself, he had certain prescriptions for others too, including the neem tree. He believed that watering in neem tree with hookah would help it grow twice as fast and make it taller and leafier. For a snake bite, he recommended for a scorpion bite.

Sucking the blood coming out of a wound caused by something sharp would take care of it. If someone met with an accident, he should be made to drink a lot of milk with turmeric powder.

For a dog bite, his advice was filling up the wound with red chillies. Grandfather was a good shooter and rode his horse like a jockey.

I am going to be 43 soon, and with all modern medical aids available today, should not be worrying about my health. If Grandpa lived for 86 years with his personal prescriptions of doubtful substance, I surely can with scientific ones!

## Let Sleeping Women Lie

When men in high office indulge in high passion, let them make sure that those who revel with them are not tell-tales.

Somerset Maugham was definitely wiser than President Bill Clinton who took "all those affairs very casually". Maugham, being wise was more hesitant. He said: "I have never yet made up my mind whether it is pleasanter to go to sleep with the kisses of a beautiful woman on your mouth or a cigarette between your lips".

Clinton's feigned indifference was severely tested after the Paula Jones episode when Dolly Browing stepped in with her disclosures.

Paula and Dolly have accused Clinton from exploitation bordering on molestation to having a 'relationship' of nearly three decades. Paula claims she can come out with details of 'typical identification marks' on the President's body while Dolly recounts how intimately Clinton 'knew' her all those years, Paula has of late, however, lowered her compensation claim.

If Clinton was a *Sahir*, he might have mused, "*Phir na kije meri gustakh nigahi ka gila; dekhiya aapne phir pyar se dekha mujhko.*" (Don't blame my belligerent glances, my Love, while again you look at me with passion!)

Well poets may spill ink. But, those who do not have this literary license and yet are born men—with brawny chests, broad shoulders, a strong upper lip, macho manner and other paraphernalia—there is a small matter to take heed of. You are bound to lose whenever you are pitted against faces capable of launching a thousand ships.

An anecdote illustrates this. Strolling leisurely in a hotel corridor, a woman opened an apartment and found a nude man changing his clothes. He was accused of being an exhibitionist.

Then when this man entered an apartment where a woman was changing her clothes, he was accused of being a peeping Tom. The moral of the episode being: Heads I win; tales you lose, especially, if it is threatened that they are going to be told.

## Abode for Ghosts

Nobody, these days, seem to be interested in talking of ghosts and witches. Apparitions and spirits don't (really) make their appearance, except in dictionaries. It is not very long ago that we heard stories of ghosts but nowadays they seem to have simply vanished in thin air. Where have our spooky and formless friends gone, is the question!

It occurs to me that, well, maybe this is one reason no ghost wants to be run over on the busy roads not only because of the heavy load of traffic and red lines in particular but also for, who knows, the police photographer who, after the mishap, may click them, and 'expose' them.

The roads are no longer safe for ghosts and spirits because almost every nook and corner has been illumined by mercury and sodium bulbs.

Then, should they have found shelter in ruined castles and buildings or deserted havelis, where the land-lady having had been issueless for a decade, died in mysterious circumstances? No. Even these structures have been encroached upon by property dealers. Haunted houses are unheard of these days, thanks to existentialist human beings taking them over.

Once upon a time the heroes and heroines in our granny's bed-time stories, who these long forgotten ghosts and witches were, did need a roof above their 'heads'; after all going by the popular belief, they, too, had been human beings only whose life was cut short by some accident.

Should the endangered species have been hibernating in the hollow stems of haunted trees or their thick and leafy branches, the environmentalists' axe could not really axe the tree-fellers' axe and even the trees being thus lessened, there seems to be no befitting and respectable place for the formless phantoms.

Wells, too, could be another habitat, a makeshift one, till moving in a proper accommodation, for the ghosts. But with the ground water level dipping down, farmers have put electric motors and pump sets some 50 or more feet deep into the wells. This must surely have disturbed the real estate dreams of ghosts. Those who were known to be giving shocks are obviously afraid of electric shocks!

What does remain then where the ghosts could hide themselves? Crevices and cracks? But these are already infested with crabs, scorpions, lizards, snakes et al which are fast becoming edible stuff for human beings at fast food jaunts all the world over.

These creatures, too, in a way belong to the ghost family, since many people are afraid of them, too. Yet, given a choice, ghosts are still a better option for me atleast for the reason that they inspire awe but not hatred and nausea.

I wonder if the ghosts have migrated to foreign lands but a question, which baffles me is the passport and visa issue. Their counterparts in the U.S.A. or the U.K. must have definitely objected to this mass refugee-like exodus from a Third World country to theirs. An American or an English ghost. I am sure, and going by the presumption that ghosts, too, have similar temperament as human beings, should have looked down upon our light and bare-footed bhoots.

And who knows, how, sheepishly our bhoots would stand before their Draculas, phantoms, and the Loch Ness monster. Not only would our bhoots only be branded as not having a scientific temperament, they would even be accused of shop-lifting. And with that vanishing capability, all the more.

I have come to conclude that the plight of our ghosts has become a concern for us all, of late. While a Maneka Gandhi would come to the rescue of animals and a Sunder Lal Bahuguna for trees, shouldn't there be bodies like an international commission of ghost rights, a weird life society and a United Nations ghost rehabilitation programme, with its headquarters at strong seismic spots on ground and air-crash-prone routes in air.

## American Discretion

IN a recent American contest, the "indiscretion" as attributed to Mahatma Gandhi and Indian gods and goddesses (remember the "You Tube dance" and "Maxim bout" ! ) may have been in bad taste, but the amount of discretion that society gives to its grassroots level functionaries is something that won our hearts during our sojourn in that country this summer.

We were then in Denver, the capital of Colorado. We set out to go for a city tour when at the ticket counter of a historical monument, we were asked to present our identification documents. We had forgotten to carry our passports and what I could flaunt to the woman on the counter was my I-card.

She recognised my photo and quipped, "An officer!" "Indian Police Service", I said with pride. With a matching glint of appreciation, she said, "Welcome, sir, and bring the lady also in." We did not have to buy tickets; instead the tour was all gratis with a guide in tow.

At an unaffordable town inhabited by rich and fashionable people, Aspen, also famous for being one of the world's top destinations for skiing, the question as to whether a “Group of five concession” should be given to us or not arose again. We were four adults besides our one-year-old grand-daughter, Anaysa. She being the fifth member, we claimed the group concession. The woman on the cash counter, having a good look at Anaysa, wrapped in a pink snow-suit then, smiled and happily conceded the desired concession.

While going in a city bus to King Sooper, a grocery store, the driver of the bus played what turned out to be an innocuous prank on us. He was a Muslim from Mumbai, and his complexion being pinkish-white, we could not make out his Indian connection. I offered three one-dollar bills for being fed to the ticket machine when he said I needed to put “Thirty dollars, sir”.

I was shocked, for that was a fare demanded 10 times more than the actual. I held my hand back when he smiled again speaking in Hindustani, “*Hota hai bhai-jaan, yahan bason main bhi chalna padta hai*!” And he allowed us a free return ride on our way back. Next day again we took the same route when on our return journey on the same tickets, the new driver said we needed to buy fresh ones. When we told him about the previous day’s journey undertaken on the same route, for the same duration and between the same stations, he allowed us his discretion.

At Glenwood Springs we reached Adventure Park through the cable cars at five in the evening. The charges being quite high, we were advised to preferably come the next day, for just an hour was left when the park would close. We wanted to visit the park, time being very short with us, notwithstanding. “Alright, in that case you can visit the park on the same tickets tomorrow as well in case you are able to find some time” offered the man on the counter.

Here again at Star Bucks, ordering *Chai* Latte for four “to go”, we enquired as to where could we find milk for the baby, since at quite a few places visited that evening we could not arrange milk for Anaysa. Lo and behold! The stewardess filled a take-away container with two glassfuls of milk and said, “You don’t need to go anywhere else. And don’t need to pay either!”

## The Bhajji-Veeru Predicament

Harbhajan Singh and Virender Sehwag were caught on the wrong foot when they had to cough out a couple of hundred dollars for wearing those odoriferous shoes that put off even the fish. The "dirty-duo" had been obviously sweating it out, till only a few days back toiling, taking on literally from head to toe the West Indians.

Accepting that the host country has strict laws on import of organisms in microscopic form so as to save their agriculture, the fact remains that in not giving in to obnoxious smells and instead applying perfumes and scents of the choicest brands, the western population and their lifestyle warrants some "treatment" here.

When the top world leaders of today speak, their arguments smack of things that send the affected—or even unaffected—on an olfactory drive, to understand the real intent behind their veiled utterances. One can smell the proverbial rat in their designs. The amount of fumes thus released suffocates those targeted to the extent of repulsion and revolt. But the western ways do have a euphemism for the "soft incense that hangs above the bough" as Keats observed in one of his poems.

The western smells of anthrax, of nukes, of gunpowder; all have fatal properties, typical of the western influence. We the Third World entities need to have a little longer nose to nose it all, particularly when a tragedy as at Bhopal occurs.

I am reminded of our pilgrimage to the place of "The murder in the Cathedral" where poor Thomas Becket, the priest himself, could not smell a rat in the evil designs of destiny, and he ultimately fell a victim to a fishy trap that was laid for him.

Just in the vicinity of the cathedral, we had the occasion of being in the Canterbury Museum, where they have brought alive all the Chaucerian characters, of the tales told by the undisputed Father of English poetry. The depiction was impressive and the curator had taken pains to create an ambience of the medieval times with the help of costumes and habitations of those times, to give a real taste to the visitor.

And then we entered a chamber that smelt as if it had not been cleaned since the fourteenth century—when Chaucer himself lived. The smell was typical of dry-dung and hydrated-haystacks having been (p)reserved for the likes of us—the visitors. The female voice coming from our headphones was prompt enough to inform us that the smell had purposely been created to allow the visitors have a "faithful feel" of the place.

Now I think in retrospection what crime had Bhajji and Veeru committed in genuinely making their hosts feel (faithfully!) that we Indians earn by the sweat of our brows and pay for the sweat in our boots?

## The Speaking Tree

HAVING jogged a bit hard in the Town Park, I stopped under the lonely, holy and aged Peepal tree to stabilise my breathing. "Hey, you humans are strange creatures!" I heard from nowhere when I looked at a pattern of falling bark on the trunk of the Peepal. "Are you a speaking tree?" I asked and observed a smile flashing on the tree-face. You may call it wooden, but I will not, since it had emotions, expressions and was enormously animated.

"You all are here everyday and still do not greet one another. Rather, you brush past as if by the side of a log, on encountering someone, menacingly brisk-walking on his doctor's advice. You seem to spare no winks and smiles for each other. You do not exchange even a kind of tokenism of your supplemental existence," the speaking tree was quite candid in his observations and expression of disgust.

"And what else have you observed about us, the human beings," I asked trying to restrict the curve of my smile when pat came the suggestion: "Now stand for a while and look at the one who is cutting corners literally and also the other one who does not go faithfully on the curved walking track and rather strays off tangent for a short cut. What for? To save some distance? To cheat oneself! Fools." The speaking tree was full of contempt at the behavior of the 'park pals' — an expression he did not agree with since he had not seen any bonding between those who come daily to walk in the park.

I stood speechless when again the Peepal nitpicked, "Now look at them. They are three of them. A man and two women in tow. I can have a bet that they will never walk from under the wire mesh shed, loaded with green creepers, but will 'bypass' it. Is it not pleasurable walking in that airy, shadowy, green arcade purpose-made only for them to have a more idyllic feel!"

The speaking tree had hardly concluded when I saw exactly the same thing happening in front of me. I chuckled and kept mum with my breathing being restored slowly but my eyes becoming heavier with inability to face the tree-face due to some kind of guilt experienced.

"Tell me something good and heartwarming speaking tree since you know it is very rare that one hears such pithy stuff," I tried to digress and seek a real philosophical intervention from the "Mighty Seer" for he might still go ahead with his banter against those who litter, spit and soil the parks, what the environmentalists call the lungs in urban habitations. "All I can recall are the stories of sweat and toil my dear!" speaking tree said with some lament laced in his comment.

"Sweat and toil? Sorry, I didn't quite follow it." I sought an elaboration. "All I wish to say is that once upon a time the farmer and tiller of this land used to sweat out here to earn his bread and spare a lot for others as well. But nowadays the likes of you sweat it out here but only seeking to maintain appropriate levels of your blood pressure, sugar and cholesterol etc. But you are still better of the lot," speaking tree said to me. "How come you are so kind to me?" I asked. "At least you are listening to me while all others pay no heed."

I took leave of the speaking tree quite pampered. But aren't great souls known to pamper and preach. Take heed O' Homo sapiens.

## Jam Jamboree

I have no reason to disagree with Haryana Director-General of Police Ranjiv Dalal when he says he develops a "jet lag" after travelling(?) through the Delhi and Gurgaon traffic snarls, although I have been immensely benefited, having been caught up in these gridlocks, very frequently. And I gainsay, jams do help reduce stress in their own peculiar way.

You learn not to give a kneejerk reaction, at even listening to the news about a repentant Musharraf stepping down to allow himself being "judicially" dealt with, since your legs are always busy with the brake-and-clutch operations. Yes, you may give in to jumpstarts, and it is good for nursing ambition, and bolster your self-esteem.

I have even heard lovers say they met for the first time caught up in a jam. Their eyes met, at the same time when their vehicles "met". And there was no looking back thereafter. Also there was no point, for nothing was visible except bonnets and windscreens. The reinforced stability in the lovers' character stood reassured, besides a tendency to fall in line, for there was no "lane cutting" or "sidetracking" possible.

Driving through the melee of a traffic jam gives you a feeling as if you are driving a world-class vehicle. You can read a newspaper, plonked on the steering wheel itself, for it may not be your turn, to turn it for long. And you may enjoy the thrill of driving a car, with automatic transmission, since you do not need to jazz up the gear, and continue with the same, even after going five feet.

Road rage has become unthinkable for me, at least. I rather exchange smiles, with the one who hits my rear with a fender (no pun intended please); now look, how humble have I become. In fact some of us regular jam-jelled have really developed a bonding, as should be expected between "jam pals". "Hi there! Still there? Wish you tortoise speed!" Zoom, vroom, zap and screech have lost all meaning for me, and I now like only a revved-up whirr, ghurr, dhum and pataak!

I have observed a change for the better, in people's attitude, and now they give way to others, while caught up in a jam. The realisation dawning on them that the straggler has come thus far, and may go no further, is altogether a different issue.

I always take calls on my cell phone, telling the caller, "it really is a good time calling me now" without worrying for the prying eyes of a traffic constable, since he cannot be seen around, for as long as the line of sight travels — yes, and who said nothing travels in a traffic snarl.

The jams have come to afford a roaring business for beggars as also the vendors. Believe me, for I have seen many behind the wheel, patronising the favorite among them. Office-going Babus now proudly claim their files move faster and that experienced jam jockeys at least should not complain of red-tapism anymore.

I have found the jam- prone areas, to be crime-free stretches, for none can dare to execute a successful robbery, and find an escape route. You can jolly well leave your handbag by your side, on the car seat, with a windowpane wide open, even if it amounts to an open invitation, for being looted at leisure.

The jam-packed bounties have made me overcome my phobia of getting suffocated if, God forbid, a fire broke out and there was no escape for me. Obnoxious fumes? My foot! I now jam care for them! And many road users may tow the lane, when I say, "I enjoy the jam jamboree." Do you?

## Balcony Babbler

Anaysa sits smug in her grandpa's lap. It is an everyday affair when the duo watches the early morning activities, from the balcony of their flat. She is just the mum-mum-pup-pup age but is a keen observer of things, taking place down below.

The oldie keeps telling the little one, "Look look, there is the kabariwala. He buys old newspapers." The grandpa then tells her about the newspaperman, "Look, there comes the hawker who hits the newspaper roll on our windowpanes. Stupid." She babbles mum-pup again.

Every morning the grandpa introduces different people to the little one—his bundle of joy. Now is the turn of the milkman, who is "never tired of mixing water in the milk he sells. Cheat of the first order. Should be hanged!" The puck throws a fulsome smile as if making fun of Dadu's disgust.

"And that gardener—the maali—he too sells the flowers to the florist in the market, depriving us all of a beautiful sight in front of us. Be-iman." The little elfin flashes an impish smile probably as an approval. All this goes on till she grows to become a chatterbox.

***Two years later...***

It's evening time. The *kabariwala* is on the door "to collect grandpa's books". Closely followed by him turns up the milkman, with a container of milk for getting his product tested, in a laboratory. Mom-Dad are surprised. Taken aback. Bewildered.

"But who told you Dad's books are for sale? And who told you that the milk you supply is unfit to drink?" They asked when the maali too shows up, with a bouquet, and grinning. Then is the turn of the hawker to put up his presence "to settle accounts since you don't want any newspapers from tomorrow onwards." "But who the hell told all of you all this nonsense?" Dad and Mom question them.

"Forgive us sir, but it was Gudia Rani!" They said with one voice. "From the balcony, she demanded of me to come in the evening and take away all her grandpa's books," said the kabariwala. "And she shouted to tell me you didn't need newspapers from the next day," said the hawker. "She almost called me a cheat and what not, hey Bhagwan, accusing that I dishonestly sold water and not milk," complained the milkman; while the gardener said, he too heard something like "Be-iman! Paaji! Chor!"

As if all this had not been enough for a mystery that needed to be solved forthwith, the neighbours too chimed in and protested, "Anaysa announced from the balcony, there was strike in the schools today that is why our children missed their classes."

Mom-Dad looked nonplussed and into each other's eyes. They burst into a peel of laughter.

Just then they saw Anaysa walk in. She was holding Grandpa's walking stick as if helping him take his steps the right way. Seeing the assembly of so many complainants, the little Anaysa ran in and hid herself behind the curtain. When told of her gremlin goof up, Grandpa lifted her in his arms and tossed, saying," You Shaitan.!".

Could this be possible! Well, if yes, I'd love to be called stupid, cheat, be-iman, chor, paaji, and all that babble swear.

# Language of the Lower Lip

I am not an expert in lip reading. Honestly I do not know what Tony Blair told media persons the other day. Or for that matter, I really do not know what the Bengal Tiger blurted having removed his shirt and waving it to the crowd some time back.

I even haven't gone beyond mere flipping through Desmond Morris's "Man Watching". However, I am not impressed with the 'stiff upper lip' displayed or exhibited, consciously or otherwise, by the emotionless Commanders, Kings and Queens, seeking to show up their 'erect and unruffled posture', either in the face of a tragedy or turmoil of another sort.

Still I can say with some sense of responsibility, since I have seen many Hindi movies of an era gone by, that the lower lip does convey a thousand unsaid emotions and feelings, ranging from pain to pleasure and to even lust as also disapproval, dejection and deftness. While the first category belongs quite endearingly to the female protagonists, the second is claimed by the male of the species.

Remember Sharmila Tagore's ability to express agony and angst with a quivering lower lip in many a movie. Whenever it was a situation when unbearable suffering was to be expressed as enacted, she employed her lower lip, eliciting an overwhelming sympathy for the character she played. Not to be left behind, Nutan and Mala Sinha also created a similar impact adding their equally trembling voice to the effort. Meena Kumari was of course adeptest of them all at the maneuvers of the arty lower lip, and for many an emotion, howsoever hidden, or explicit with thin concealments.

And remember Madhu Bala playing Anarkali in Mughl-e-Azam, who sought to entice Prince Saleem played by Dilip Kumar, in the all-time great number, *Pyar kiya to darna kya*, by repeatedly tucking and releasing one side of the lower lip between her teeth. This (obviously! God knows for what!) lusty and lecherous expression on the face of an actress, never inviting the Censor's scissors coming to play, was surely a double take on the solicitous overtures of the women of easy virtue of those times, on whose predicament Guru Dutt made the magnum opus Pyasa.

Sadhna in Inteqam, while singing *Kaisay rahun chup ke maine pee he kya hai*, avails herself of the protruded lower lip with a rounded upper one uttering "tch-tch, tch-tch" to tease Rehman who had wronged her in the past. A protruded and flattened lower lip, always suggests disapproval while the slightly projected upward one is associated with making fun of the subject.

I remember another string from the movie Arpan made in black and white, on Gautama Buddha. Here it is a dance sequence when the female protagonist tries to entice a meditating disciple of Buddha. In the scene he remains seated 'unseduced' till the time step-tapping and drums make him bite his lower lip. Blood then trickles from there thus completing the display of a tenacious hold in his character yet laying bare the effect of enticement on a man by a woman. The dancer also then gives up her effort.

What do you say of the lower lip now? Lose, placid, ludicrous or lustful!

## Gutsy Girlie

My orthodox, hard-boiled Haryanvi grandmother would have committed suicide on hearing the news about Bhuri Kalbi's daughter, surviving a premature birth, slipping through the toilet bowl of a running train near Ahmedabad, in Gujarat. Also, she would have been not at all pleased with tidings from Bangalore about three-year-old Laxmi, surviving a surgery involving separating two of her extra limbs, around Divali last year. "It's only the chhoras (boys) whom death and disease like to visit and not chhoris (girls)", was her eternal lament.

My grandmother would also have caught by the neck Dr Alexander Jacob, the Director of Kerala Police Academy I visited recently, for how dare he take pride in boasting, "Out of the sixteen-hundred women recruits, we have 400 postgraduates, including 47 doctorate holders and the rest 1200 are graduates."

The in-flight experience on my way back had a weakling in me exposed inside out on my "gender sensitivity" — sensitisation can be taught. Minutes before the takeoff, the air hostess maneuvered hard to close the door when it swung swiftly off the latches. The engineer, a young Sikh, was sent for, who fixed the door. Only thing required was to use some extra muscle and a hard push.

Leaving instructions with the airhostess, he went out to see if she could close the door herself from inside. She could not; but was undeterred in her resolve to do the job trying umpteen times. Foolishly we kept fastened to our seats. Lending a helping hand to the damsel might also not have been appropriate for she had to learn to be enough plucky. When she finally closed the door, all passengers on board clapped.

After about an hour of being airborne, the plane hit turbulence. The passenger occupying the window seat in our row indulged in a kind of self-reassurance saying, "Shouldn't he have stabilised the plane by now?" "It is not a he, but she! Didn't you hear the Captain's announcement in a sweet voice?" I quietly whispered into his ears. All through the flight this man kept praying with his seat kept in upright position and making restless body movements.

Having touched down at New Delhi and the plane being in taxi mode, I had a mischievous but mild dig at my friend, "Was it not a very smooth landing!" "That's alright but could she have shown enough mettle and grit in case, God forbid, the plane was hijacked?" "Have you washed off your memory the sacrifice of Neerja Bhanot, a flight purser on a Pan-American flight, who laid down her life in 1986, rescuing three children and was posthumously awarded the prestigious Ashok Chakra?" I reminded him. Shame was writ large on his face when he looked at me, grinning.

## Argument on Wagah

While driving past Amritsar to Wagah, we had thought we would experience all that should be different. People, soil, food, dwellings, crops, language, etc. Also, we'd thought everything should look, as between worst enemies, torn and divided: culture, community, ancestry, history and religion. But that was not to be.

We had heard about the drill at Wagah and the sentiments attached to the event. A colleague in my office had once told me, "One is very enthused and enough prepared to die for the country at that moment, Sir". The Indian side shouts "Vande-Matram, Bharat Mata ki Jai and Hindustan Zindabad". The other side says, "Pakistan Zindabad, Paaindabad. Lowering of the flags on both sides is followed by a common drill in which the Border Security Force men and Pakistani Rangers "outstep" each other with overt and aggressive, macho display of strength.

Well we reached the Wagah border with barbed fencing leading from both sides. The strong iron-gates were painted in tricolor scheme on "our" side and green & white on "theirs".

Crowds of people having patriotic blood flowing through their veins had gathered on both sides. Each half was charitable but only to itself in shouting slogans. It was here that I felt there existed two countries, two people, two communities, two entities.

But still carried away by my fondness and respect for our mutual bonhomie with Pakistan, the tales of which I had heard from my father and grandfather, I began cheering even the "other side" when they sought response to their sloganory exhortations. Suddenly then, I felt a tapping on my shoulder by "someone". I turned back and looked someone with whom an argument ensued reflexively.

"Why are you cheering them?"

"There is nothing wrong in that"

"Are you one of those?"

"And are you someone different?"

"Don't know they're separate now?"

"Do rivers stop entering this side?"

"Political rhetoric is long dead"

"So will be peace-willing generations!"

"Khushwants, Nayyars, Asma Jahangirs?"

"Yes. Precisely. So let's cheer each other."

"Don't you hear they swear by Allah?"

"Large number among us also does that."

"They're under seize and are tensed."

"That's why they deserve our cheers!"

"Emotional fool! Go your way"

Having been thus rubbished, I realised that "someone" was none else than my own flawed self.

But what I had been looking in that crowd, even after the event of retreat drill, was the face of a child called Noor. Remember she had a successful heart surgery in Hindustan some years back. I am sure the likes of her would be the new generation in Pakistan.

The Retreat left me more hopeful. Emotional fool. Did you say that? No. Now it is “someone” again at it. Damn him and hail peace!

## Chosen Ones

Who doesn't want to be rich and famous? And who won't like to pool all the resources at one's command to be in the hall of fame? Since all of us cannot make it to that status, do we not seek identification to impress the world about our acquired level of superiority? But destiny is somewhere there, playing its quiet role.

Lady Luck doesn't smile on everyone. You have to be a "chosen one" to have that divine favour; boon or benediction. Hitting a jackpot, winning a lottery, being the millionth buyer of a car and getting it free, or stumbling on a hidden treasure, are all in the hands of God. Or providence, if you prefer that word.

There may be other parameters to judge one's being lucky or unlucky. Being fortunate and being successful are two different things. Fortune favours while success succeeds. One may wait for Lady Luck to smile but one has to really be in a hurry and strive to be successful. Skills, of course, do make a difference in shaping one's destiny. Also if you are possessed with the ability to bend your bones or pull a truck by your eyelashes, it does make a difference.

Epics, sagas, tales, episodes, incidents, instances are mostly made up of stuff that providence provides and protagonists possess. Yet a fair or unfair distribution of what is perceived as booty makes one lucky or otherwise.

Indian films provide enough material on divine allocation of resources. If a starving hero saves the life of a rich man, or still better, his daughter, then he mostly has the best of both worlds. Remember Ifteqar in "*Deewar*", who places his bet on a shoe-shine boy who grows up to become Big-B, saying, "*Ye lambee race ka ghora hai* (He will go a long way in life)." While in the first case, it is being lucky, and in the second, successful.

There may be many ways to be rich and famous. Some people do name-dropping and proclaim and clamour about their relationship with the already rich and famous. For example, you can always find characters who brag about, saying, "I have direct access to 10 Janpath!" or "Madam recognises me in a crowd!" Those who are not able to make it to Bollywood in any recognisable way can be seen dropping names like "Ramu is dependable!" or "Vidhu is just like a younger brother!"

By way of a reverse argument, if you at least verbally take on the might of a biggie and pose a challenge to his authority, you become one of the debated ones. Heard of that couplet from Zafar Gorakhpuri, "*Kitni aasani se mashhoor kiya hai khud ko; Maine apne se bade shakhs ko galee dee*!" (How easily have I made myself popular by simply abusing someone really great?)

You can think of various ways to be in the news at least, if not rich enough. Come in the way of a wealthy man's car but do please avoid Salman Khans. Also if you are able to survive an air-crash, train accident or a boat capsizing, when all about you are gone, you definitely make the stuff when curious journalists could be seen interviewing you, almost gagging your mouth with that instrument which they call an ID, "How are you feeling now?" or "How really do you feel now, when the entire world knows you?" True, some are born great while others strive and gyrate. Sorry, Mr. Shakespeare!

# Send Them to Coventry

To "send someone to Coventry" means making him feel his redundancy. The expression has a historical background also. Churchill ignored warnings for the bombardment of Coventry by the Germans, to save London, as a tactical move.

The other day, casually flipping through half a dozen newspapers, my friend said to me: "Nothing really exciting!"

"What happened? There is enough there to be just happy about!" I contorted mischievously when he said, "Complacence, isn't it? Can't we send them all to Coventry?"

"Whom?" I asked. "To begin with the likes of you—Cops!" he concluded with all the contempt hurled at me and my tribe.

And he unfolded his intent to banish all the policemen of the country to the "Island of the naked" to learn passive resistance, a la Gandhi, having no temptation and situation, when they should be able to rob anybody of their belongings. "Leeches all!" he said.

"And what about you, journalists? Should they all be not packed off to jungles where being unable to sneak into private lives of people, they cannot sting others, but get stung by wild scorpions, snakes and black widows?" I said and quizzed my friend, winking, if he had any solution for the politicians.

Presto, he propounded a wonderful idea. "These moral lepers be made to spend a year or two in universities and Centres of Excellence to improve their qualifications?" I quipped poking fun at my friend's proposition but he said matter of factly, "No! For the simple reason that they should learn how our academicians fight—and on issues that are so trivial that put to shame even the infants in their pans."

"Look buddy, this gives me enough food for thought and I suggest that all our Blueline drivers should spend at least a fortnight sleeping in a mortuary; the Gen-X brats be bundled off to old age homes to hammer a point in their psyche that they themselves would grow that old and infirm," I philosophised.

"Makes lot of sense!" my friend exclaimed and with his tongue firmly in his cheek said: "Let all the lawyers go to Pakistan, where they can learn to really fight."

"What about the religious bigots?" I asked and my friend had a ready answer: "To the abattoirs and butcheries where they may have a change of heart and develop aversion to spilling blood."

When this tete-e-tete was going on, I flashed back to the time when I myself was once sent to Coventry. We were taken to downtown Coventry from where we strayed into some sidelanes. Here we encountered some junkies and one of them tried to snatch my camera.

We looked for the cops around but were later told that even for the police that was a “no visit area”. Was it really a part of our training to feel the helplessness of a victim? Or, were we to know the real meaning of being “sent to Coventry”, I still wonder.

Having returned to myself from my fanciful flight, I urged myself to make a point, “And ...!” But I was checked by my friend, “Hold on dude, for everything else the Judiciary hai naa!”

## More than What Meets the Eye

TO be able to read between the lines means the clairvoyance to comprehend what is actually intended to be conveyed. But how about going micromillimetres distance between the canvas and the brush to identify as to how many layers of visuals rest there? And also that, what exactly should one pose in a portrait show-up? Isn't it all really mystifying? It may be true! It may be false!

An Italian scientist-journalist by the name Piero Angela claims to have discovered Leonardo Da Vinci's self-portrait, by going down the surface of a manuscript — Codex on the Flight of Birds, employing a micro-pixel work. A facial reconstruction scientist in Rome has even endorsed Angela's claim. What is interesting is the fact of the "resurrected" Renaissance genius's young looks, appearing twin-like when compared to his portrait showing him up in wrinkles, and with hollow cheeks.

Another world famous portrait of Renaissance, "Mona Lisa", created by Leonardo, has been in the news for various interpretations, inter alia, of the pose of the wealthy merchant's wife. That she wears a thin and gauzy stole around her neck, confirms her being in a family way, going by the mores prevalent then. That she is hiding her pregnancy with one hand above the other also confirms it. Arguments are too many, but takers some.

The latest to hit the market is the news about an Anglo-Irish family, preserving Shakespeare's portrait inherited from the Earl of Southampton, showing him with not only younger looks, but also betraying his humble background and nowhere-near-wealthy status. That having moved to London and having written his famous plays, the Bard of Avon grew popular and wealthy in the Elizabethan times, made him look more "presentable and less solemn" if one has to believe Shakespeare "experts" and "scholars" .

Nearer home, the National Dairy Research Institute at Karnal has come out with five rare photographs showing Mahatma Gandhi with a cow named Jill. Pandit Madan Mohan Malaviya is also seen in one of the pictures. Claims have been made of the photos taken when Gandhi attended a two-week course at the institute to learn the basics of dairying and keeping cows, for his Sabarmati Ashram.

The latest revelation has been made regarding the legendry Bhagat Singh's photo, taken shortly before his hanging, for keeping it in records. A portrait showing Chandra Shekhar Azad, twirling his moustache in front of a mirror, is again disputed if it had been a replica of the original photo taken without the martyr's knowledge.

I cannot help mentioning about a movie, "Lage Raho Munna Bhai", showing the redoubtable and inimitable Boman Irani to be someone obsessively interested in doctoring his life-size images, as if "actually" standing for a pose with celebrities. And for that matter, of all times! Who knows five hundred years from now, someone may come up with a theory that Boman was a President of the United States and Obama played character roles in Bollywood flicks.

However, what Ben Johnson says in commendation of the Martin Droeshout engraving of Shakespeare is worthy of taking note: "This Figure that thou here seest put/It was for gentle Shakespeare cut... His face; the print would then surpasse/All, that was ever writ in brasse/But, since he cannot, Reader, looke/Not on his Picture, but his booke".

## For Whom the Bell Tolls

Press the doorbell if you hear sounds suggesting domestic violence. This message is being conveyed through an advertisement on the TV these days. It may appear to be intrusive, yet it checks the extreme execution of anger. Wise people say if you push the ungainly moment into eternity just one time, it may not come back to you with the same tight-fisted intensity.

It so happened during our initial years in service that in the Officers' Colony, we had someone ring the doorbells at odd hours. None was found around on enquiry. The mysterious act continued for days altogether, creating a kind of fear among the families during those grim days of terrorism. Across the fences, in the driveways and over the boundary walls, we discussed as to who and to what end would dare to torment the officers and their families for nothing.

One summer evening, I and my wife were sipping coffee after dinner in the dimly lit lawn with Chander Prakash and his wife. We saw our neighbour A.K.Garg's house carefully bolted on all sides, including the main gate, besides the entry to the flat. The Gargs seemed to have entrenched themselves in a kind of fortification. We could see their pet sitting on his haunches in the balcony. We collectively decided to play a prank to have fun.

Executing the conspiracy, I told my orderly to go home after ringing Mr. Garg's bell, and that of M.K.Mahajan, and two other officers in tow. He grinned demurely, knowing pretty well the consequences. He also knew we would backtrack on his abetting by us. But as the cops would always go for the kill if it amounted to some adventurism, he agreed.

Almost as a "non-state actor", we saw him vanishing in the dark after pressing the Gargs' doorbell, to further carry out his assigned task. With controlled whispers and gagged giggles, we began to watch the goings-on in Gargs' compound.

The windows started to light up one by one. The pet rose to the call of duty perhaps to cover up his not raising hell when a familiar "stranger" had sought a sneak. The door opening into the balcony made a creaking sound while Mr. Garg appeared there with genuine apprehension but bold disposition, saying it loudly and forcefully — "Kaun hai! Arre bhai kaun hai?" Like an apparition and in tow, appeared a visibly scared Mrs. Garg.

Mr. Garg saw us from the balcony and yelled, "Deswal Sahib,aaj hamri ghanti baj gayee!" All the four of us feigned ignorance and assured the couple that we had been sitting right there, and did not notice anyone coming near the house. "Moreover, Brownie, too, was fairly alert". We tried to be clever by half.

A hypertensive Mrs. Garg almost began to faint. My wife realised the gravity of the situation and promptly whispered the conspiracy plan into Mrs. Garg's ears. Thankfully, she instantly smiled, holding her head in both her hands, more to relax herself than to be amused.

While we were there enjoying the aftermath of a successful stunt, we saw M.K. Mahajan arriving on the scene with his wife and three-year-old daughter. His carrying a steel curtain rod, twice his size, though threatened us initially, but all was well soon.

Next day it was our turn to turn down our orderly's "dossiers" sent to us by the neighbours. Surprisingly, the doorbells stopped ringing in our colony thereafter.

## Tana-Tunn

Slangs may be more tolerable and less sober. With sufficient amount of faithfulness, sincerity and honesty, they convey the intended message in perfect tone and tenor. This undoubtedly makes the conversation more enjoyable.

Hindustani slangs' list may be exhaustive, but let us have a look at some of these colloquial expressions. Consider Tana-tunn first. Enquire about someone's health and he may quip, "Tana-tunn!"

Now there are a thousand meanings that can be attributed to this argot. Tana-tunn may connote a "condition", "position" and so on. Generally, it is an overstatement made when (and mostly) it comes to one's potency or inadequacy, or both.

Mall does not refer to Mall Road or Shopping Malls only. The slang means everything, ranging from merchandise to even someone you may have a crush on. More so when it comes to the supply of betel leaf, footwear, cosmetics, fabric, medicine, machinery, screws, anything or everything on earth, including "kidneys", the dispenser may say, "*Mall hi nahin aaya*!"

Take for example our own indigenous jugar. It means an alternative, when the actual is unavailable. Jugar encompasses "virtually" everything that "works"; be it a government, a machine, a system or even an improvisation. In the Indian context, jugar may be a stop-gap arrangement, which can be "dragged" on without inviting frowns, and with impunity.

Phoonk remains my personal choice ever since I became conscious of my ego. You assume airs and inhale enough phoonk. Others also make you inflate with phoonk. In case of a failure, they always refer to some kind of a deflation of phoonk only; but then they will say, "Sahib ki phoonk sarak gayeei" I don't know if it is a pointed adaptation to "taking wind out of the sails!"

Sho-sha is again exhibitionist in character. It is a gimmick. A prank. A trick to lure. Blandishments. All combined to make one indulge in an impulsive ostentation, or showing off. Sho-sha entails expenditure, and is considered dispensable for the critics, who call it extravaganza. Sho-sha is feed for some, and food for many.

Fukrapan relates to one's style. Of dressing. Of talking. Of one's conducting oneself, in a manner generally perceived to be a fetish, fixation, mania or obsession. Fukrapan also takes its toll on the practitioner's expenses.

In a Rajesh Khanna movie of the seventies, I was shocked (then) to hear him call his soul-mate a Kutti Cheeze—a hurricane, or a bewitching beauty! These days they use callings which in due course have become "acceptable". They may relate to "wear" and "tear" — no pun intended, please.

We are middle writers. Kutti may be a bitch, and cheeze (also vastu) may mean more than that cheesy white stuff.

Bindaas is someone who is bold, from out of the world, adventurous, overbearing, go-getter, and what not. The late Devi, a woman journalist who used to write gossip columns, coined this expression which may, no doubt, one day find place in Oxford and Macmillan dictionaries. Other slangs from Bollywood include Mamu, Beedu, Dhakkan, etc.

Last but not the least to mention is tahsan. Finer and even bolder nuances of this slang connote something done as a precursor to another thing which has the force of a firm belief, be it religious, personal or societal. For example, if someone distracts at that very moment when the die is to be cast, then they say the tashan is lost.

Remember the successful gimmick of "Yaaran da tashan" in an Amir Khan advertisement of a popular brand of cold drink! What? Did you really comment on my pen? Well, it is tana-tunn! No pun intended please. We are middle writers!

## O' to be Obamas' Dog!

I woke up in the wee hours to eavesdrop on a unique canine conference. The venue was my backyard where nearly all the elite breeds of dogs were represented. They seemed to have unleashed themselves from all mundane shackles from the nearby houses, using their sixth sense.

The issue of "Who to be Obama's dog?" was being fiercely debated in dog-eats-dog projections, about suitability of various breeds (read races), to gain entry through the Pearly Gates of the White House. In the chair was my own St. Bernard, appropriately called, Haider.

An Alsatian opened the plenary with the doggerel: "I am His Majesty's dog at Kew. Pray Sir, whose dog are you?" "Hey you! Basically German (Shepherd)! Likes of you may not be preferred in the U.S.," said the Staffordshire Terrier and added an all-too-acidic comment on even the hitherto silent Doberman, "You too. The one given a name after that blood sucker tax collector, in Germany."

Not to be put down easily, both of the German breeds growled in a kind of jugalbandi when a Cocker Spaniel interjected, "We are more acceptable in the U.S. Remember the most popular language in that country these days is Spanish!"

"Stop all that nonsense on races and languages," intervened the black Canadian Labrador from Newfoundland, "Didn't you hear Obama likening himself to a mutt — of mixed breed."

At this our own street dog Sheroo, sitting doggo all this while, stretched his limbs, turned his head away from the deliberations, and started singing *a la* Dilip Kumar in the movie "Sagina Mahato" — *Bhole bhale lallua khayeja roti baasi; bara ho ke banega Sahib ka chaprasi!* (O' my innocent child, keep on eating stale food, you will definitely grow up to be a peon, in attendance to an officer, one day.) None paid heed to Sheroo's ecstatic outpouring dubbing it uncouth and enough desi.

"O.K., Okaay. No one needs to be a Pekingese Royal, theft of whom carried death penalty in 18th century China," said a Chihuahua of Mexican origin. "You be quiet there. Sacred and edible stuff for the Red Indians! Don't deserve to be dogs! Bow wow!" barked in the American Bulldog. "Remember we are the ones, after whom the dogmatic reassurance came from some human fella — The more I see of man, the more I love dogs!" said he, "And it suits us fine. But we need to act fast for Peru has already offered their breed 'Ears' from Incas to Obama."

While all this was going on, I saw Sheroo cozying up with Tikki, a white exotic female. Turning away from the deliberations, I lent my ear to what Sheroo had to very endearingly tell an "expecting" Tikki. "Aey sweetheart, crossbreds of whatever shade have a safe future in the U.S., and our ladle and ladlee — little ones — to be born soon, will surely find their way in the White House, for they will be hypoallergic mutts, as also the bald variety, suitable for Obama's daughter Malia, who is allergic to the fur and hair."

I don't know whether the canine conference reached a decision with all that bar (ac) king or not but the duet Sheroo and Tikki sang, while walking away from the dogged venue, still reverberates in my ears, confirming the sanguineness of the couple's American dream — *Jeevan ki bagia mahkegi, lahkegi, chahkegi; Khushiyon ki kalian, jhoomengi, jhoolengi, phoolengi!* (Our life's flowerbed will experience fragrance, blossoms and flourishing; Our happiness buds will experience swaggering, swinging and thriving.)

## Call of the Unknown Soldier

Driving past Maj. Sandeep Shankla Park in Panchkula, I hazily saw certain Army and private vehicles lined up, in a thick downpour. It was some solemn ceremony going on. Army men were slow-marching with wreaths, to the bust of the officer, who gave his life in the line of duty, on August 8, in 1991.

Moved and impassioned, I told my driver to take the first available U-turn. Memories of the Kargil War flashed on my mind, when I had witnessed six soldiers "brought-home-dead," in Fatehabad District alone.

Brave people of this region are known, not only to take in their stride, the loss of their men going down fighting, on borders for the motherland, but also to feel the collective pride of the sacrifice made by their valiant sons. I can recall the skies ranting with slogans of "Amar Rahe" and "Jab tak Suraj-Chand rahega, Foji tera naam rahega".

The mother of one of the soldiers, who when she saw the District Magistrate and the Superintendent of Police, offering with their salutes to be the pallbearers themselves, had commented, "O' son, you have repaid me the debt of my milk!" None cried, albeit all around looked grim at the loss of the one who brought them glory. On his son's last journey, the father had said, "I have the whole lineup of my sons if the country needs them!"

Thousands, cutting across caste, race, colour, religion, sect and ideology had gathered at the last rites. They seemed to follow only a patriot's religion then. Military honours done, a long lineup of mourners offered floral tributes to the departed son of theirs. Volleys of shots echoed as if from the hearts of people around and the Last Post was sounded. The pyre was lit by a three year old, the martyr's son, when some folks seemed to have lost control over their emotions.

The driver brought me back from my memory lane on reaching the Memorial site. Some civilians carried umbrellas as it was still raining. I alighted from my car to be received with dignity by a couple of smartly dressed officers. Straightaway, I was accosted to the bust. Carrying the floral wreath, which I was supposed to place at the bust of Major Sandeep Shankla, two more men in ceremonial dress joined in ahead of me. And I too began to march.

Something in me ignited my whole self. I was, as if, spiritually energised and blessed. With every step on climbing up to the bust, I felt a lifting out of myself. An alleviation of sorts! No sad thoughts in mind but those of gratitude, indebtedness and obeisance! I offered the wreath. Prayed for the man for a while. Saluted the soldier. And with matching agility, infused in me then by the ambience, I turned right to step down.

Back in the car, I recalled to myself words inscribed under the bust of Martyr young Lieutenant Arun Khetrapal, who laid his life to the call of duty, having just then passed out of the Indian Military Academy, in the 1971 War with Pakistan, “When you go home, tell them of us, that we gave our today, for their tomorrow”.

My driver asked me if I had personally known the soldier. “No!” I said and pondered if I’d said the right thing. Soldiers are known to generations of men and not a few of them. The call of the ‘Unknown Soldier’ can command you to “About Turn,” should you chose to forget him. Remember this! Remember him.

# Dating Advice to Vijender

Sex symbol Bipasha Basu's offer to date Olympian Vijender Singh may have been taken as a spirited backing- up gesture, when the pugilist needed it the most, but it has also drawn flak from certain quarters, in the tradition-bound state of Haryana.

Even the bronze winner boxer himself has reportedly "gone back on Bipasha" saying if only she hadn't had any "boy-friends"! And that he needed to concentrate more on his punches than crushes. Now don't flex those muscles John!

For us Indians, dating amounts to a misadventure in sex, while in the West, it is nothing but a close or first encounter, of two willing beings, mutually seeking to explore each other with no limits premeditated, for a future 'course of action'. Even the parents are known to be guiding their children on their first date.

Likewise, as an officer superior to Vijender (Remember both of us have Haryana Police to boot), I can imagine a situation when I will guide my young friend, presuming that he has had offers from many a Bollywood girl, and given that, Vijender is not in the serious "game of dating".

And true to his pulisia blood, he is not supposed to pay, the ones who seek to date him.

For someone like Rakhi Sawant, Vijender is well advised to take along 50 politicians (take care, list of those interested may be a tall one) so that they can finetune the fine art of loud mouthing. He should take precaution not to go too close to her.

If the Olympian Cop has a call from someone like Katrina Kaif, then he should take along 50 "keen-to-learn-Hindi" school students to inspire. Diamonds may be forever, but not the dates-like Aish.

Let some two score well-fed couch potatoes accompany the boxer if he gets a dating call from someone like Vidya Balan. She can inspire these obese brats to trim down a bit to be in shape for at least refresher parties.

In case of an Antra Mali, the man should take along as many dull heads as he can, who lack ambition in life, for she can make a small fry dreaming to become a Madhuri Dixit.

If Vijender hasn't had enough of media handling then he shouldn't say no to a dating offer from Priety Zinta who can send them all on the back foot. A hundred underfed kids should accompany him to a date with Shilpa Shetty who has enough booty from U.P. and Bihar, as also London.

Priyanka Chopra can tell him during a date how to court two "suitors" at a time and this will enable the pugilist to fight more than one challenger. For this he can also try a Kareena who can guide him into moving for a "nutty candy over a Chocó one"- accepting challenges, I mean.

This otherwise shy and hesitant boxer should pick up some killer-instinct laced knocks from Urmila Matondkar or Kajol. Should Vijender be in a mood to change his coach, then he needs to go on a date with Archana Puran Singh or Kashmira Shah.

Neha Dhupia again holds promise being a closer-home Delhiite. The more innocuous ones like Diya Mirza, Deepika Padukone, Koyna Mitra, Malaika Arora, Gracy Singh, Amisha Patel et al, too may have some "acting" or "modelling" tips for Vijender.

Am I missing out on someone from Haryana? I shall restrict myself here, for Gotras, are a serious business in Haryana and can land you in the almighty wrangle of a panchayat. To hell with the silly imagination! I never said anything.

# HOLYPOL